"Excellent. Will Sarni and Greg Koch have taken on the challenge to set out in clear and practical terms how strategic forms of multi-stakeholder collaboration can help governments and policy makers strengthen their governance of wicked problems like water resource management or the food–water–energy nexus. They succeed with clarity and finesse. Packed full of useful examples and interviews *Creating 21st Century Abundance through Public Policy Innovation* is a smart, cogently argued and easy to understand analysis of what innovative partnerships look like, why they matter and how they can be used to help policy makers address our systemic natural resource challenges. With the delivery date for the Sustainable Development Goals now just 12 years away, Sarni and Koch provide a perfectly-timed proposition of how a platform of partnerships for the goals can actually be built."

Dominic Waughray
Visiting Scholar, Stanford Woods Institute for
the Environment, Stanford University

"'Business as usual,' is a state of mind, and this is generally the way humanity looks at water. Obviously, this is the wrong approach. Will and Greg have managed to analyze very clearly the weak points of the water sector and to highlight the necessary steps needed to be taken in order to correct it. This book is a 'must' for every person that is concerned with our future."

Oded Distel
Director, Israel New Tech & Eco Systems

"In an era when amorphous water risks are becoming profound realities, make no mistake, lack of action in the boardroom will leave companies adrift and exposed to potentially devastating disruptions. With masterful narratives and revealing context, William Sarni and Greg Koch guide readers through tumultuous waters, providing historical grounding and clear channels for the critical decisions ahead. In *Creating Abundance*, readers will learn how to set bold goals, apply best problem-solving skills, and have faith in the collective abilities necessary to embrace the challenges ahead. We live in a new world where water is the metaphor for survival in business and in life. In this important and accessible work, Sarni and Koch align the value and values that will separate success from failure."

Carl Ganter
Co-founder and Director, Circle of Blue

"Equitable water governance is the linchpin to addressing most of the water challenges we face. Will and Greg have drawn on their extensive pioneering experiences in the corporate water stewardship space to elucidate concrete ways we can all work toward this goal."

Jason Morrison
Head, UN Global Compact CEO
Water Mandate

"This thought-provoking book opens with the premise that the singular water strategy we've been pursuing for centuries – 'let's go get more water' – needs to be set aside in the 21st century so that we can move into the real work of trying to figure out how to find true security and well-being within the limits of water availability. These two authors – who have spent their lives working on water challenges around the globe – offer rich perspectives on the innovation that we need so urgently, and they've tapped a deep well of stories that illustrate the way forward."

Brian Richter
President, Sustainable Waters

CREATING 21ST CENTURY ABUNDANCE THROUGH PUBLIC POLICY INNOVATION

One of the greatest challenges of the 21st century is the problem of how the public and private sectors can sustain economic development, business growth, social well-being and ecosystem health in the face of accelerating demand for water, energy, and food. "Business as usual" projections of scarcity in water, energy, and food predict a lack of these resources sufficient to sustain economic and business growth as well as an adequate standard of living worldwide.

Developments in technology are well documented, but this is the first book to explain the role of innovation in public policy and governance, a topic which is frequently overlooked and often frustrates developments in technology and business. Without innovation in public policy and governance, innovation in technology solutions will face persistent headwinds for adoption. The book showcases these innovations and creates a roadmap of what needs to change to drive economic development, business growth, social well-being and ecosystem health in the 21st century.

William Sarni is an internationally recognized leader on water strategy and innovation and CEO of Water Foundry, Colorado, USA. He has authored numerous publications and presented on the value of water, water technology innovation and the energy–water–food Nexus. He works with multinational companies, NGOs and startups.

Gregory Koch has some 30 years of experience and is a globally recognized leader in water resource management and water stewardship. Formerly, Greg led The Coca-Cola Company's global water stewardship program where he collaborated with bottling partners, governments, NGOs, aid/development agencies, and communities across the world.

CREATING 21ST CENTURY ABUNDANCE THROUGH PUBLIC POLICY INNOVATION

Moving Beyond Business as Usual

William Sarni and Gregory Koch

Routledge
Taylor & Francis Group

LONDON AND NEW YORK

First published 2018
by Routledge
2 Park Square, Milton Park, Abingdon, Oxon OX14 4RN

and by Routledge
711 Third Avenue, New York, NY 10017

Routledge is an imprint of the Taylor & Francis Group, an informa business

British Library Cataloguing-in-Publication Data
A catalogue record for this book is available from the British Library

Library of Congress Cataloging-in-Publication Data
Names: Sarni, William, author. | Koch, Gregory (Water management
    specialist), author.
Title: Creating 21st century abundance through public policy
    innovation: moving beyond business as usual / William Sarni
    and Gregory Koch.
Description: Abingdon, Oxon; New York, NY: Routledge, 2018. |
    Includes index.
Identifiers: LCCN 2017054788| ISBN 9781783538096 (hbk) | ISBN
    9781783537518 (pbk)
Subjects: LCSH: Sustainable development. | Social responsibility of
    business. | Environmental policy.
Classification: LCC HC79.E5 S266275 2018 | DDC 338.9/27—dc23
LC record available at https://lccn.loc.gov/2017054788

ISBN: 978-1-78353-809-6 (hbk)
ISBN: 978-1-78353-751-8 (pbk)
ISBN: 978-1-351-04290-1 (ebk)

Typeset in Baskerville
by Swales & Willis Ltd, Exeter, Devon, UK

William Sarni
To Maureen, James, Thomas, and Charles for your support and enduring belief that *we will* make the world a better place.

Gregory Koch
To Johann Koch.

CONTENTS

LIST OF FIGURES AND TABLES

Figures

Tables

ACKNOWLEDGMENTS

Thank you to Piper Stevens, Matthew Wheeland, and Deanna Marie "Drai" Schindler for their contributions to the interviews, manuscript, and graphics.

ABOUT THE AUTHORS

William Sarni

 Will is an internationally recognized thought leader on water strategy and innovation. He has authored numerous books and articles and presented on: the value of water, innovations in digital water technology, the circular economy, and the energy–water–food Nexus.

He has been a water strategy advisor to private and public-sector enterprises and NGOs for his entire career. He has worked with multinational companies across a range of industry sectors in evaluating the technical viability and market potential of innovative water technologies, market entry strategies, and M&A programs.

He is the author of: *Corporate Water Strategies* (Earthscan 2011, and in Chinese by Shanghai Jiao Tong University Press 2013); *Water Tech – A Guide to Investment, Innovation and Business Opportunities in the Water Sector* (Sarni, W., and Pechet, T., Routledge 2013); and *Beyond the Energy–Water–Food Nexus: New Strategies for 21st Century Growth* (Dō Sustainability 2015). He is currently working on the forthcoming book, *Water Stewardship and Business Value: Creating Abundance from Scarcity* (Sarni, W., and Grant, D., Routledge 2018).

Will is a Board Member of 10.10.10 (www.101010.net) and ASSET (www.assetcampaign.org) and Founder of WetDATA.org. He was a 2016 X-PRIZE Bold Visioneer for the Safe Drinking Water Team and is on the Scientific Program Committee for Stockholm World Water Week; Executive Council of NOAA's National Integrated Drought Information System (NIDIS); Editorial Board of the *Journal of Water*

Security; and a Technical Advisor for the Climate Bonds Initiative: Nature-Based Solutions for Climate and Water Resilience.

He is from New York City and lives in Denver, Colorado.

Gregory Koch

Greg has nearly 30 years of experience and is a globally recognized leader in water resource management. From 1996 to 2017, he was employed by The Coca-Cola Company where, as Senior Director, Global Water Stewardship, he led the strategy and direction for Coca-Cola's global water stewardship program focusing on: water use efficiency and wastewater management in production facilities; watershed protection and climate change adaptation; community water and sanitation supply initiatives; supply chain water management; global awareness and action; and water policy engagement. He collaborated with bottling partners, governments, NGOs, aid/development agencies, and communities throughout the Coca-Cola system.

Greg is a board member of the Global Water Challenge.

He is from Germany and lives in Atlanta, Georgia.

At the time of writing, the author Greg Koch was employed by The Coca-Cola Company as Senior Director, Global Water Stewardship. Mr. Koch wishes to inform and acknowledge that he did not write this book as a representative of or on behalf of The Coca-Cola Company, and that the statements, thoughts, conclusions, opinions, etc. expressed in the book are not necessarily those of The Coca-Cola Company. Instead, they are those of the author personally.

FOREWORD

by Stanley A. Motta, Chairman of Copa Airlines,
Latin America Conservation Council member

When I was growing up my father taught us and often repeated that there were two things in life people did not appreciate until they do not have them: health and freedom. Today I think he would add a third, WATER.

This book deals with what is a complicated subject and outlines what can be done to either narrow or eliminate the "water gap." Most of us are fortunate enough to turn on the tap in the morning and not have to worry about where the water comes from or its quality. Obviously, climate change is important but more significant is the fact that if you believe it is coming quickly, slowly, or not at all, most of what needs to be done has to be done anyway.

Most of the water we use we do not drink but eat, as the largest use of water is for agriculture, so we need it to survive and to also provide a healthy environment in which we live. Water is also unevenly distributed not only by regions of the world but often even within a country and during different seasons. The book makes clear that the technical knowhow and resources exist to make the situation better, but one of the questions the book helps us understand is who owns the problem. The answer is simple, we all do.

If countries want to grow and provide a better life for their citizens, the economic management of water will be essential to the future. Water is no longer just an issue for the environmental and social ministries but one the ministries of economic affairs, trade, and commerce need to incorporate into their planning. Business is well on its way to understanding the importance of water to their enterprise and to the communities where they operate but they alone do not have the resources, and nor are they the correct entity to solve the problem.

I often use the expression that if "everyone in the room is losing their mind" while trying to understand a situation "and you can remain calm, it's because you do not understand the situation." In today's world, there are no "silver bullets" to make our problems go away and if we look at recent history, only collaboration has worked to really solve the big problems of the past or invent the tools we need to help solve them. Collaboration needs to be led by someone as there is no time for accidental events to lead the way. We all have governments to help us solve the collective problem and while they should take the lead it is up to civil society and business to make sure they do. Regardless of your present role in society, water needs to be on your agenda. Its impact in our lives and the lives of others is not difficult to understand, and it is not impossible to mitigate or solve the problem.

Experience has taught me that knowing a subject is important but even more important is knowing how to put the right people in the room and then to make sure everyone has the patience to reach a consensus, patience being the important element.

This book will teach the reader the importance of water, its many aspects, and hopefully raise interest in solving a solvable problem. It also addresses ways to implement the collaborative solutions needed, to achieve the Sustainable Development Goals, and, as we face the "Nexus" of food, energy, and water security, to give us the opportunity of creating abundance.

INTRODUCTION

The test of our progress is not whether we add more to the
abundance of those who have much, it is whether we provide
enough for those who have little.

Franklin D. Roosevelt

Franklin D. Roosevelt made this statement on January 10, 1937 in
his second US presidential inaugural address.[1] Those words rang
true 74 years later when, in November 2011, Greg attended the first
global conference dedicated to exploring the challenges faced by
the nexus of food, water, and energy (the "Nexus"). The conference was sponsored by the German government and held in their
former parliamentary setting in Bonn, Germany.

From the end of World War II, until after the fall of the Berlin
Wall in 1989, this amphitheater and surrounding office complex
was used by the German government as the city of Bonn became
the capital of a new country, West Germany, with the old capital of
Berlin in the hands of the Russians in East Germany.

Once Germany reunified and the capital was once again in
Berlin, the United Nations made good use of this complex to
house the "other headquarters" with a presence they always wanted
outside of the UN complex in New York.

Why Bonn, why Germany, and why the focus on the Nexus in
2011?

The German government paid close attention to output leading to a seminal report[2] from the World Economic Forum's Global
Agenda Council on Water Security which identified the Nexus as
a – perhaps the – defining sustainability challenge for the planet.

Changes to achieve growth or security in one category can exacerbate or even create problems where none existed in one or both of the other components of the Nexus.

An example is the government subsidy and mandate in North America for biofuels. This is unquestionably a noble pursuit, for cleaner forms of energy as well as some measure of energy independence. But with this policy, maize grown to be converted to ethanol went from a single digit percentage to over 50 percent. This energy security initiative has in turn led to a historic rise in the cost of maize (a food security issue), and water and land stress, even in water-abundant places. This dilemma exists almost everywhere.

Another example is the overuse of water supplies to increase food production, limiting downstream hydropower production, as well as water supplies for cities and ecosystems. A comprehensive set of literature on the Nexus can be found, including co-author Will Sarni's book *Beyond the Energy–Water–Food Nexus: New Strategies for 21st Century Growth* (Dō Sustainability 2015).

It was fitting to host the Bonn Nexus conference in the former government complex, as both the meeting complex and the topic were powerful symbols of dramatic change. However, the Nexus presents a fundamental change in how we must look at and solve problems; there is no "Berlin" to return to. Most nations, perhaps the planet, are approaching or are already at finite limits: How much carbon we can put in the atmosphere, how much water we can take from the environment in a given time and place, how much we can pollute, and even how much debt (government and personal) can be sustained?

We already have or likely will reach other limits for further resources, processes, and systems due to emotion (e.g., yuck factor for wastewater reuse), policies (conflicting), structure (how we organize corporations, government agencies), academia (how and what we teach), and society/culture (what we value).

Another limit is self-imposed, mainly from bias. When we talk of growth and security (water security, food security, civil security, etc.), whose security are we talking about? When we talk about security in the Middle East, is this for those citizens or the West? When we talk about water security, is this for a country, a corporation, industry, agriculture, or nature?

Having neared or reached such limits, Earth-bound mankind will for centuries, if not forever more, be faced with a challenge to achieve abundant growth in the absence of abundance.

You might wonder how the Nexus trumps global warming and climate change, the scourge of disease, poverty, and so many other societal, economic, and environmental challenges. A fair question and certainly open for debate. Climate change and population growth, in particular, are massive "force multipliers" in further complicating solutions to existing problems, creating entirely new ones (sea-level rise, for example), and inserting uncertainty and unpredictability. What's more, climate change is already underway, having significant impacts, and will devastate much of what we have built and value. Climate change is emblematic of how the Nexus has risen to become the challenge we will face.

However, it is the authors' joint opinion that the Nexus is indeed the challenge facing all of us. We purposely omitted the adjective "sustainability" before "challenge" as that often seems to place the discussion in the realm of a "nice to have" or "feel good" mostly environmental-resources arena. Perhaps the central observation in all of this complexity is the rate of change, in water supply and quality, food and energy demands and availability, all in the context of siloed planning and execution across the Nexus.

We feel that a shift in thinking is necessary.

Most debates or negotiations related to water start with the premise, on one or both sides of the table, of "more." How can one user, conservationist, country, farmer, or industry get *more* water for their use. Thus the discussion begins in a state of conflict with solutions driven by someone getting "less" and/or supplies of water being increased to meet higher demands.

This concept of "more" is prevalent throughout most of society. What politician does not speak of more development, more jobs? What investor does not expect more profit? What industry does not want to grow more business?

In the Bonn conference, plenary debate became heated discussing how to increase, achieve more. A lone voice, a man from the Philippines, asked why we are so focused on financial and development well-being (economic growth?) and not on human and natural well-being. It was a powerful moment that created a silence, a pause to reflect.

Growth cannot be infinite yet growth is needed, to restore unhealthy ecosystems, eradicate poverty and gross income inequality, end hunger and malnourishment, and so much more. Is a focus on well-being versus growth the answer? The moral and ethical perspective certainly supports well-being: growth must include equity in access to resources, the "democratization" of access to energy–water–food.

We believe, and this book attempts to show, how a focus on well-being with the right public (and corporate) policy can lead to solutions and abundance in the face of limits. This is a solvable problem. However, this does not mean that everyone gets everything they currently want and in the way they plan to achieve growth. There are tough choices to be made.

Other tough decisions include wholescale changes in academia, government and corporate organizations, and in civil society, which will take time. Like any complex and complicated problem, you take one step at a time.

Chapter 1 illustrates in detail both how current approaches have caused many of our current problems and how such approaches, even with the best of intentions, will not work for the future.

Chapter 2 further defines the Nexus and bridges that complexity to the myriad of singular issues we are already grappling with. Chapter sections outline the demand for resources, along with population growth, in a rapidly changing climate.

Chapter 3 completes the foundation of our problem set in examining the types of tough choices that need to be made, as well as the many factors that make decisions to execute a tough choice so difficult.

Throughout Chapter 4, we focus on solutions, the opportunity to achieve abundance and well-being. This includes several success stories from the innovative public–private–civil society collaboration, to transform policy toward Nexus security and growth by the 2030 Water Resources Group.

The Sustainable Development Goals are also highlighted as individual and collective means to achieve growth and abundance, but also show how new ideas on linking efforts between certain goals and prioritizing some goals over others can actually speed up progress and even lower costs.

Reducing vulnerability and increasing resiliency will round out the chapter, discussing innovation, technological and otherwise, and showing how a focus on these "enablers" will improve the human and ecosystem capacity to cope with the changes and difficult choices to come.

Chapter 5 provides our thoughts on the way forward – a roadmap to creating abundance. We believe abundance can be created through innovative strategies that break down the energy, water, and food silos, coupled with harnessing the creativity of entrepreneurs.

In this introduction, we have presented a daunting situation. We do not posit that the solutions and way forward we present is the only answer. However, we hope this book provides concrete paths toward growth, well-being, and abundance, starting with a shift in thinking.

Notes

1 Franklin D. Roosevelt, "Second Inaugural Address," January 1937, www.bartle by.com/124/pres50.html, accessed November 12, 2017.
2 World Economic Forum, "Water Security: The Water-Energy-Food-Climate Nexus," 2011.

1

THE PROBLEM WITH
"BUSINESS AS USUAL"

Business as usual is killing us. But, as Alfred E. Neuman is often quoted, "What, me worry?" seems to be the prevailing attitude.

When the supply of resources vastly exceeds demand, there is little to no need to focus on the efficient and effective use of these resources. This has been our collective view for a very long time.

Unfortunately, demand now exceeds supply and we are failing to manage energy–water–food effectively and for the long term. The result is that we have an ever-increasing population with large segments without access to safe drinking water, energy, or proper nourishment.

Let's abandon business as usual.

We can and must deflect the scarcity trajectory we are on by *implementing* innovative public policy, technology, financing, partnerships, and business models. It is possible, and, as you will read later, actually occurring.

First, how did we get here?

Population growth is driving increased demand for energy, water, and food. This is further complicated by the negative impacts of climate change. This is our new normal and as a result, old practices and beliefs will no longer serve us well.

For example, there is a lack of knowledge concerning water risk throughout the public sector. Our 19th and early 20th century policies are no longer sufficient for innovation, as they do not consider water stewardship programs that are crucial for the continuation of economic growth.

In order to implement new policies, it is important to analyze the effects of water scarcity *before* changes are made. Business-as-usual projections yield the need for adjustments, and the complex and interrelated nature of the water, food, and energy sectors prove that programs should be focused in these areas. Public policies and business initiatives should seek to engage external stakeholders while quantifying the value of water.

Business growth is dependent on resource availability. Critical resources include energy, food or agriculture, and water. If a business cannot maintain access to these resources, its progress will be stunted and profit will be affected. In the *VOX Global/Pacific Institute Report*, a study showed that 79 percent of responding companies admitted that water challenges are currently prevalent, and 84 percent predicted the presence of water challenges in the next five years.[1]

Water scarcity does not solely impact the water sector, but also the energy and agriculture sectors. The water–food–energy Nexus is crucial in understanding the value of water and the impacts from global warming. Corporations will need to implement policies in order to compensate for the changing availability of resources. This can be done through water innovation, with a focus on stakeholder ecosystems, technology, and business or financial modeling.

Risk associated with business-as-usual practices

Due to the global population growth, changes in demand for water, energy, food, and urbanization, business-as-usual practices will not be sufficient for the future. The International Union for Conservation of Nature (IUCN) estimates that by 2050, the water, energy, and food demands will increase by 55, 80, and 60 percent, respectively.[2]

The global population is currently increasing by approximately 70 million people each year. As a result, the total global population is projected to reach 9.6 billion by the year 2050.[3] This growth will increase the pressure on limited water, energy, and food resources. Energy consumption is estimated to increase by 1.6 percent each year, amounting to an increase of about 36 percent by the year 2030. Additionally, pressure on agricultural resources will increase through societal habits such as consumption of more livestock and vegetable oils. The number of calories that a person ingests each day is expected to increase from 2,373 kcal/person/day in 1969/1971 to 3,070 kcal/person/day in 2050.[4] Urbanization will yield more industrialization and water usage, and the water demand will increase from 4,500 billion cubic meters to 6,900 billion cubic meters by the year 2030.[5] This estimation assumes that the efficiency in water technologies does not improve, and *the projected demand is about 40 percent over our currently accessible and reliable supply.*[6]

Demand for energy

In the Organisation for Economic Co-operation and Development's (OECD) 1999 report on energy in the next 50 years, energy demand is characterized by electricity, mobility, and stationary uses.[7] The demand for energy is expected to increase especially due to non-OECD countries' projected increase in population, higher living standards, the transition between non-commercial and commercial fuels, and urbanization.[8] In OECD countries, demand is also expected to increase as electricity and mobility expand through a rising gross domestic product (GDP).[9]

The United States Energy Information Administration (EIA) projects a 48 percent increase in global energy consumption by the year 2040.[10] Renewable energy and nuclear power are expected to increase by 2.6 and 2.3 percent, respectively, each year.[11] Non-fossil fuels are

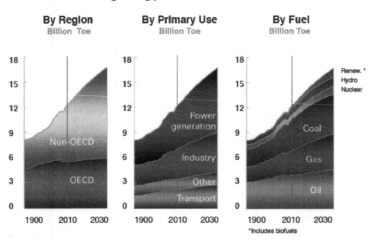

Figure 1.1 **Projected energy demand growth by region, industry sector, and fuel type to 2030, in tons of oil equivalent (toe)**

Source: BP, *BP Energy Outlook 2030,* January 2013.

predicted to grow faster than fossil fuels such as petroleum, natural gas, and coal. Natural gas is expected to increase by 1.9 percent each year, while petroleum-based liquid fuel is estimated to decline to only 30 percent of the "liquid's share of world-marketed energy consumption"[12] by 2040 (see Figure 1.1). Consumers will begin to prioritize more efficient technologies as oil prices increase in the future.

Demand for food

By 2050, the demand for food is expected to increase *between 59 to 98 percent.*[13] As a result, crop production will need to be increased. Crop production can be improved through greater land use for agricultural purposes or improved efficiency in irrigation or other farming methods. Although it may seem that these solutions are available and fairly straightforward, there is concern when considering land use.

Today, approximately 50 percent of the world's habitable land is utilized for farming. In fact, agricultural processes account for 38 percent of the world's land area.[14] There is a finite availability of land for food production, and it is expected that the land use in developing countries will increase by 120 million hectares in order to meet additional food demands from the growing economy and population.[15] In these circumstances, natural ecosystems that cultivate wild plant and animal species are being replaced by large monoculture regions, which have an intensive demand for water and energy.

Unsustainable agricultural practices additionally limit the availability of land for food generation by desertification: 12 million hectares of land per year are left barren and unsuitable for agricultural use.[16]

Demand for water

The World Economic Forum claims that "roughly one-third of the world's population now lives in water-stressed areas, and nearly a billion people still live without access to safe drinking water."[17] The drought is enhanced through the overdrawing of underground aquifers in regions such as California's Central Valley, the North China Plain, northern India, and America's Great Plains.

A landmark report from the 2030 Water Resources Group (WRG) report, *Charting our Water Future*, provided a very clear view of water scarcity, both globally and within selected regions.[18]

This is Will's "favorite" line in the report – "There is little indication that, left to its own devices, the water sector will come to a sustainable, cost-effective solution to meet the growing water requirements implied by economic and population growth." The report makes the key points that, in the world of water resources, economic data are insufficient, management is often opaque, and stakeholders are insufficiently linked.

This also sums up the challenge of the water–food–energy Nexus and the public policy (and technology) challenges we face.

WRG maps out scenarios for water supply and demand and frames a "water gap" on a regional scale. Actually, there will not be a gap – *there will just be difficult allocation decisions.* Assuming there is a "gap" – it will be the pain that drives how businesses and the public sector address their risk and opportunities.

It is worth repeating that the report concludes that "by 2030, assuming an average growth scenario and if no efficiency gains are realized, global water requirements will grow from 4,500 billion cubic meters to 6,900 billion cubic meters – about 40 percent above current accessible and reliable supplies." This statement has been quoted more than often. Figure 1.2 from the WRG report illustrates clearly this "gap."

Agriculture is the bulk of the global water demand, with current (2017) use at about 71 percent of total demand. By 2030, the WRG expects that:

> agriculture's total water use will increase, but with faster population growth its share will decline slightly to 65 percent of total demand. Industrial demand is currently 16 percent, with a projected increase to 22 percent by 2030. Domestic water demand will decrease slightly from 14 percent to 12 percent by 2030.

The focus of WRG is on closing the gap – historical improvements in water efficiency in agriculture returned only about a 1 percent improvement between 1990 and 2004. There has been a similar rate of improvement in the industrial sector. If we project these efficiency improvements to 2030, we would only meet about 20

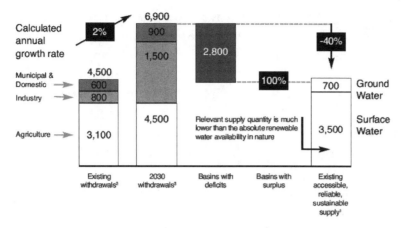

Figure 1.2 **Projection of water supply and demand by 2030**

1 Existing supply which can be provided at 90% reliability, based on historical hydrology and infrastructure investments scheduled through 2010; net of environmental requirements.
2 Based on 2010 agricultural production analyses from International Food Policy Research Institute (IFPRI); considers no water productivity gains between 2005–2030.
3 Based on GDP, population projections and agricultural production projections from IFPRI impact-water base case.

Source: Adapted from WRG, *Charting Our Water Future: Economic Frameworks to Inform Decision-Making*, 2009.

percent of this 40 percent "gap." If we assume a 20 percent increase in supply, we would still have a remaining 60 percent of demand that is unmet. Not a great scenario.

A few of the other conclusions from the WRG report:

- Agricultural productivity is a fundamental part of the solution to closing the water gap since the agricultural sector makes the greatest demands on global water use and water efficiency is one of the key low-cost technology solutions.
- Industrial and municipal productivity are just as critical as agricultural productivity improvements.
- There is a link between quality and quantity of water.
- Most solutions require cross-sector tradeoffs, such as increased irrigation to promote agricultural productivity and resultant increases in energy use.

The briefing report by the 2030 Water Resources Group for the World Economic Forum 2012 Annual Meeting includes additional research on the issue of water scarcity currently and projected for the future. Currently, over 70 of the world's major rivers are already so "over-allocated that little of their water actually reaches the sea."[19]

What we face if we don't manage energy, water, and food is a lack of access to those most basic of human resource needs. If this is the choice we make, we will confront the familiar consequences of starvation and poverty and a lack of water. We have seen it before: the collapse of civilizations.

"Business as usual" is not an option.

Notes

1 Will Sarni, *Fueling Growth: You Can't Always Buy What You Need*, Deloitte University Press, 2014.

2 International Union for Conservation of Nature, "*The Water-Food-Energy Nexus: Discussing Solutions in Nairobi*," May 28, 2013.

3 Will Sarni, *Deflecting the Scarcity Trajectory: Innovation at the Water, Energy, and Food Nexus*, Deloitte University Press, 2015.

4 Will Sarni, *Beyond the Energy–Water–Food Nexus: New Strategies for 21st Century Growth*, Dō Sustainability, 2015.

5 Ibid.

6 Ibid.

7 Organization for Economic Co-operation and Development (OECD), *Energy: The Next 50 Years*, 1999.

8 Ibid.

9 Sarni, *Beyond the Energy–Water–Food Nexus*, 2015.

10 US Energy Information Administration (EIA), *International Energy Outlook 2016*.

11 Ibid.

12 OECD, *Energy: The Next 50 Years*, 1999.

13 Maarten Elferink and Florian Schierhorn, "Global Demand for Food Is Rising. Can We Meet It?" *Harvard Business Review*, April 17, 2016.

14 McLellan, Richard, "Farming: Habitat Conversion & Loss." *WWF*. Web.

15 Ibid.

16 Ibid.

17 Ganter, Carl, "Water Crises Are a Top Global Risk." *World Economic Forum*, 2015. Web.

18 2030 Water Resources Group (2030WRG), *Charting Our Water Future: Economic Frameworks to Inform Decision-making*, 2009.

19 2030WRG, *The Water Resources Group Background, Impact, and the Way Forward*, 2012.

2

THE CHALLENGE OF THE NEXUS

Greg's 10th-grade high school algebra teacher, Diane Ash, made clear that "You can only solve for three unknowns with three equations." This basic lesson in mathematics serves as a fitting frame to explore a few observations about the scope of the challenge in addressing water challenges across the Nexus, both today and in a changing climate.

Number 1: When you engage most governments on water security issues, you will find varying levels of understanding of the problems, the effectiveness of the existing policies they employ to manage water resources, and the capacity to implement these policies. Capacity is critical and consists not only of sufficient staffing and experience, and sufficient funding, but, critically, the proper level of authority. Too often, water resource management is fragmented and even subservient to other policies and ministries.

Number 2: These challenges are daunting but can – and are – being addressed in many places, as awareness and response to water risks continue to rise. However, the authors have repeatedly observed that trying to solve water problems cannot succeed if the focus is only on water. Most nations, perhaps the entire planet, are approaching or already at finite limits for carbon creation, water use, pollution, and even debt. This stress of limits has intertwined water, energy, and food security to a high degree of complexity. *A good decision to address a challenge in one area can create a new problem in one or both of the other areas.*

The Nexus presents a multivariate problem. If we take a basic algebraic viewpoint we quickly see that you need three equations to solve for three unknowns.

Number 3: We are not organized to solve for three unknowns. This begins in higher education, when we train water engineers, agronomists, and energy experts. It carries on into how we organize government ministries into separate silos – water, agriculture, energy.

Corporations are similarly organized. Even most of civil society (non-governmental organizations or NGOs) are largely single-topic focused. The embedded hierarchies, politics, and vested interests in such organizations pose a complex and complicated scenario.

Number 4: All of these challenges are amplified when you step into a transboundary water setting. There are, of course, many legal and practical issues in such settings but recognize that transboundary water challenges are not only surface water and ground water at a border. Many of the water stresses the world faces stem from the virtual transfer of water. Consider land "grabs," large tracts of land in southern Africa under cultivation of crops for export to China. This virtual transfer is also evident in the export of cotton and other crops from northwest India, olive production in northern Jordan, but also in significant ground water stress in the American southwest driven by long-term contracts for the cultivation and export of alfalfa and related products to China and the Gulf States.

All four of these observations certainly present a unique predicament. That predicament is negatively amplified by a changing climate that is today having real impacts but also has much unpredictability.

Changes are driven by a warming climate along with growing populations and greater development and even higher incomes. These factors, when layered on top of the four observations presented above, lead to the conclusion that it is not just the present-day complexities that we must focus on, nor only the projected ultimate changed state that is predicted once populations, economic growth, and climate change stabilize (if they even can). *It is the rate of change that presents the greatest challenge.*

Demand for resources

The Nexus stress is limiting economic development, business growth and social well-being. As the Indian agricultural scientist

M.S. Swaminathan stated, "*If conservation of natural resources goes wrong, nothing else will go right.*"[1]

This is the bottom line.

Let's translate the Nexus stress into actual impacts.

Nexus stress and limits to economic development

Although it is easy to analyze the impacts of each sector on an individual basis, public policies for innovation should acknowledge and utilize the water–food–energy Nexus when developing financial and stakeholder ecosystem models. The Nexus introduces the concept of interdependency between water, energy, and agriculture.

Joppe Cramwinckel of the World Business Council on Sustainable Development (WBCSD) states that, "Water, energy and food are intrinsically interrelated: A sustainable solution for one almost always has an impact on the others."[2] Water is needed in order to produce energy through fuel production, thermoelectric cooling, and hydropower, while energy is needed to source, treat, and transport water.[3] Agricultural processes require both water and energy, which are influenced by drought, and could increase crop prices.

Additional economic implications arise when discussing electricity prices if the presence of water is drawn down and companies modify thermoelectric technologies: the price of electricity will increase.[4]

Countries like Brazil and China are already having to deal with economic impacts of the water–food–energy Nexus. In 2015, Brazil had a projected 0 percent economic growth rate, with a potential for an additional 1 to 2 percent reduction.[5] China's industrial water use is heavily reliant on the acquisition, processing, and burning of coal, which amounts to 20 percent of all water consumed.[6] Since China is the largest producer of hydropower globally, Chinese rivers will not be able to accommodate an increasing demand. Additionally, agriculture in China will be exposed to risk. A combination of dry land and inefficient irrigation practices affects the vulnerability of China's food supply, and a lack of understanding or awareness of the Nexus will negatively impact China's production in the future.[7]

The economic effects of the Nexus are also depicted in the United States. Specifically, California is influencing business growth and stakeholder relations. Due to the competition for water after water-limited conditions arose in California, the governor issued a mandatory rationing of water for the preservation of agricultural, energy, commercial, and residential use.[8] The drought was expected to hit California's economy with a US$3 billion loss in 2015. Jobs are also threatened; 17,000 jobs in the agricultural sector were lost in the year 2014.[9] Desolate land is becoming more apparent, and 500,000 acres were bereft in 2014.[10] In terms of the energy sector, prices are proven to be rising. In 2014, ratepayers spent $1.4 billion more for electricity than in previous years. As opposed to utilizing hydropower, water scarcity prompted California to switch to natural gas, which can be held accountable for rate increases.[11]

The scarcity of water is amplified through a concept known as the "tragedy of the commons." This idea arises through the nature of water as a shared resource, which makes it impossible to establish ownership. It is difficult to control water access due to public policies, regulations, and stakeholder ideals. An example of these restrictions can be seen in the availability or lack of a social license to operate.[12] The World Wildlife Fund (WWF) identifies water as a complex public resource, and it is necessary to analyze trade-offs between corporate interests and basic human rights.

In order to encourage innovation to decrease water-related risk and cultivate opportunity, corporations must consider the Nexus when addressing business and economic growth and social prosperity. In November 2011, "The Water Energy and Food Security Nexus: Solutions for the Green Economy" conference developed a water, energy, and food policy, which established methods for conquering Nexus stress.[13] Various stakeholders such as the World Economic Forum, WWF, and the International Food Policy Research Institute supported the platform and other strategies are evolving today.[14]

Nexus stress and limits to business growth

Businesses are already experiencing the impacts from the water–food–energy Nexus stress. Companies like Volkswagen, Sekisui Chemical Co., Ltd., and Mars have reported higher water prices, which results in risks manifested as higher operating costs or a reduction in revenue.[15] Water scarcity risks associated with corporations can be from physical, regulatory, community, reputational, investment, and geopolitical risks.[16]

Physical risks for businesses deal with water shortages, surpluses (flooding), and pollution.[17] In many countries, there is a lack of infrastructure capacity to transport and deliver water and wastewater, which adds secondary risk to corporations. In two African cities, SABMiller has experienced physical water risks through threats to supply and reliability. In Dar es Salaam, Tanzania, saltwater has intruded 20 boreholes, which are used for the company's operations. Additionally, in Polokwane in South Africa, the brewery has "faced deteriorating reliability and quality from the municipal water supply."[18]

Regulatory risks involve restrictions placed by the government on water use. The variability of water licenses and regulations due to physical or political implications relates to a business's water risk.[19] The arid region of Almeria in southern Spain exemplifies these effects. Business risk has increased through over-allocation of ground water, and the local government was stagnant in the alteration of prices of water consumption. As a result, retailers like Marks & Spencer have insisted upon water efficiency and stewardship practices.[20]

Community limits or risks create volatile social, political, or regulatory ecosystems, which impact employees or create supply chain disorder. As conflicts emerge around access to clean water, "companies may be blamed by local stakeholders because they provide an easy target,"[21] even if they are not directly responsible for the problems at hand.

Along with community risk is reputational risk, which influences stakeholder involvement. Customers may decide to no longer purchase a good or service due to a company's water consumption or reputation. Even if a business does not directly deal with a specific body of water that is of environmental concern, any correlation between the two, through a company's supply chain or operations, could negatively influence one's reputation. The area of Plachimada in the Palakkad district of the state of Kerala in India is mainly dependent on ground water resources for irrigation and domestic use.[22] As demands for water increased throughout the community, more boreholes appeared, yet the local government allowed Hindustan Coca-Cola Beverages (HCBL) to utilize 0.3 and 0.6 million liters of water daily.[23] Protests against the HCBL plant began, and many blamed the plant for the decay of ground water availability. The plant has been closed since 2004. Around this time period, with a comprehensive, plant-level risk assessment across its global system, informing a strategic response, Coca-Cola has implemented a water stewardship program for all of its plants.

The next risk relates to investment, where water-related disclosure policies will be required of investors and retailers. The WWF expects these requirements to occur through formal accreditation, water stewardship standards, and disclosure metrics.[24] The Carbon Disclosure Project (CDP) launched the CDP Water Disclosure Initiative, whose focus is on providing the global market place with water-related data from corporations. Through the CDP Water Disclosure Initiative, investment risk and commercial opportunity can be clarified as investors determine which companies they will invest in. HSBC and Standard Chartered have already developed position statements on the influence of water-related risks in the decision-making process.[25]

Finally, businesses may experience geopolitical risks, which relate to social or political conflicts around the allocation of water or trade restrictions. The changing climate will amplify these risks, and "water sharing, energy pools and food trade between countries on large rivers"[26] are all factors relevant to business growth. Many Asian countries and Gulf states have already bought or leased areas of land and water in developing countries, with hopes to secure access to food or water resources. In water-stressed river basins, competition will become apparent, with the potential for armed conflict.[27] For instance, South Korean interests in water leases in Madagascar have been argued to be one of the causes of the recent coup. The UN Secretary General Ban Ki-moon even attributed the conflict in Darfur to rivalry over water resources.

These water risks can be experienced on the individual–business level and through shared risk. An example of shared risk is depicted through the horticulture industry in Lake Naivasha in Kenya. As the population and demand increase through foreign exchange and job opportunities, cultural and ecological sectors have been affected.[28] Pastoralists have had limited access to the lake and farmers "have been accused of over-abstracting and degrading the ecologically important lake."[29] Therefore, European customers have been encouraged to boycott Naivasha flowers, which introduces shared risk into the private and public sectors and for European retailers.

If nothing is done to mitigate these risks, business prosperity will be affected. Even if a corporation is not directly involved in the water industry, it can still be influenced through indirect or shared risk. New regulations and efforts must be incorporated into business models and public policies, or the risk will only increase due to climate change.

Nexus stress and opportunities for business growth

Nexus efforts must include a water stewardship platform. Water stewardship differs from water management, as water stewardship focuses on "how competition for water might affect business continuity, brand value, and license to operate."[30] Water management is a specific component of water stewardship and only looks at the effects of water scarcity on direct business costs. Efficiency is the driver of water management, while *innovation* is central to water stewardship.

Three aspects of effective water stewardship practices are preservation, engagement, and innovation. Preservation refers to the mitigation of water related risk through a decreased water demand. The common strategy for water preservation efforts is to increase water efficiency and quality. Appropriate methods for reaching these goals are on-site wastewater reclamation and reuse, rainwater harvesting, technologies that limit the amount of water delivered, and restricting unintentional water loss such as water leaks.[31] The associated risks that are reduced through increased efficiency and quality are "water-related business disruptions, potential compliance obligations, and pricing."[32] Companies can also increase their reputation through actions of water preservation.

Ford Motor Company initially focused on water efficiency and quality as part of its water stewardship strategy. Initially, manufacturing operations reduced water used by cutting back in percentage increments. Later, stakeholder and community involvement were used to enhance the water policies.[33] Additional research such as water footprint calculations and targeting water-stressed regions were the beginning of the next step of Ford's water stewardship program: engagement.

Engagement focuses on stakeholder relationships, and encourages the public sector to look into water-related issues that they do not directly control. Examples of impacts that involve stakeholders, and, therefore, corporations, are "upstream water quality, supply chain risk, potential new regulations, license to operate, and reputation."[34] The involvement with outside stakeholders is referred to as "collective action," and is crucial in water stewardship policies.

There are a multitude of opportunities and risk-mitigating factors related to collective action. The Nexus is a "wicked problem" (discussed in greater detail in Chapter 4); it can't be solved alone – multiple stakeholders must engage to address complex Nexus challenges. Various stakeholders include local communities, government officials, NGOs, regulators, investors, customers, suppliers, and competitors, as long as the discussion is based on water use and management for organizations.[35] Specific examples of water-related stakeholder engagements include out-reach programs for safe drinking water, reclamation structures such as wetlands, modification or additions to water infrastructure, joint research, and annual sustainability reports.[36]

The management of supply chain risk and maintenance of license to operate are two important goals that a corporation must consider. In order to decrease supply chain risk, organizations can require suppliers to maintain a level of efficiency throughout the manufacturing process. Additionally, risk can be mitigated through working closely with individual suppliers or customers.[37]

Scenarios that highlight water risk due to scarcity are even seen in regions of high rainfall. Businesses can be exposed to risk through public policies, political agendas, and lack of funding. In the case of one rain-intense country, risk was manifested as a lack of funding. A local business consumed more water than was needed to receive development funds, and its water supply was cut off.[38]

License to operate can take on a literal and figurative meaning. In some cases, license to operate can be socially constructed, so it is vital to engage applicable stakeholders in a water stewardship process. Intel's success in Chandler, Arizona, validates this approach. Intel wanted to build a semiconductor fabrication plant, which was water-intensive. When Intel engaged the community, a water efficiency policy was developed which recycles up to 75 percent of the water used by the plant today.[39] Intel also built a ground water recharging system, designed to treat and reuse at least 3.5 billion gallons of water.[40] As a result of Intel and the community's collaboration, Intel was able to manage its water risk in an arid location, cultivate growth, and manage economic losses.

The final step to an effective water stewardship policy is to create opportunities through innovation. Innovation can be achieved by corporations who deal both directly and indirectly with water. Although water scarcity may not seem correlated to Intel's line of business, the company has developed a "Water Wars" simulation in conjunction with Sandia National Laboratories. The simulation highlights their 3-D imagery and modeling capabilities while also encouraging stakeholder involvement in water conservation efforts.[41]

Many benefits are reached when multiple organizations unite to achieve a water-related goal. Several bottling companies have depended on Ecolab to innovate on their behalf. After Ecolab created a "new line of conveyor belt lubricants that decreases the amount of water needed for bottling and canning operations,"[42] efficiency and conservation goals could be reached.

Another example is the collaboration between The Coca-Cola Company and Coca-Cola FEMSA, its largest bottling partner in Latin America.[43] Coca-Cola FEMSA has invested in 32 water funds, investing capital from downstream water users to finance upstream water stewardship.[44] Contributions from corporations, utilities, and other water users have amounted to $27 million, and are paying for reforestation projects and rural small business development projects.[45] As the focus remains on "green infrastructure," costs associated with "gray infrastructure" can be lessened. A decreased risk of reduced water quantity or quality also results through collaborative and innovative water conservation and stewardship methods.[46]

The four stages of water strategy maturity

Preservation, engagement, and innovation are specific approaches within water stewardship practices that should be considered when developing public policies related to water scarcity. These approaches are typically more general, and specific models can be used to channel the concepts of preservation, engagement, and innovation into overall business and public policy strategies. In order to link growth with water availability, there are four stages or models that the public sector can follow in water conservation or management goals. It should be noted that water risk management will impact the availability and vulnerability of the water sector directly and *also* the agricultural and energy sectors through the Nexus described previously.

In order to be able to describe the four models for maturity between public policies and water availability, there must be an initial model, Stage 1, which relates to "business as usual" methods. In this stage, there is no stakeholder engagement, limited water efficiency investments, and a lack of correlation between water stewardship and business growth.[47] Water scarcity is not recognized as an imminent or serious issue, resources are not weighed by their availability, and the market price of water dictates business and policy decisions. Here, water scarcity is not deemed an issue and corporations are willing to pay the variable price of water, as it is assumed to be a commodity and externality.[48] As a result, "this approach is sustainable only for resources whose current and future abundance are beyond question."[49] The impacts of maintaining a Stage 1 water strategy are also amplified by climate change, and will be discussed later in this chapter.

The second stage is the "efficiency strategy," which focuses on water efficiency. There is still a lack of stakeholder engagement, and the price of water is a motivator for actions.[50] The value of water, which is economically quantified through costs and intrinsic value, is not considered in this stage. The "efficiency strategy" acknowledges the applicability and extent of water scarcity issues, and utilizes this information to dictate costs. The cost of the acquisition and use of water in business practices is also accounted for. Efforts in this stage are typically restricted to an individual basis, and efficiency, savings of cost, water reuse, and water recycling are all motivators. For many corporations, the "efficiency strategy" is the "first step toward viewing water as a platform of growth."[51]

Incorporating stakeholder engagement, Stage 3, the "risk strategy," deals with a social license to operate and manages water scarcity risks on an internal level.[52] There are targets set for efficiency and reuse, even though there is "limited understanding of the value of water as a driver for investment decisions to support growth."[53] The engagement of stakeholders reduces water scarcity risks and the potential for water-limited conditions to invoke business constraints. Access to water through stakeholder relations is hoped to improve, as the systematic nature of water is understood. Water availability is assumed to be uncertain for the future, and sustainability is incorporated into an effective business strategy. In this stage, public policy formulation may begin and there may be some investments in technology innovation.[54]

The fourth stage of the maturity of a water strategy is the "license to grow" stage. Here, companies focus on long-term growth. Rather than ignoring the true value of water, it is quantified and included into current and projected business models. There is an emphasis on the maturity and refining of efficiency and reuse initiatives, and stakeholder engagement expands to the enterprise level. This water strategy is aligned with a business growth strategy, and corporations are proactive in the development of water-related policies.[55] There is large investment in corporate level technology innovation, and, as opposed to a "social license to operate," Stage 4 utilizes a "social license to grow." The concept of collective action is embraced, which can give a company a competitive advantage and drive participation and practice.[56]

In order to promote the maturity of water stewardship programs and public policies, the shift from a Stage 1 or 2 strategy to a "license to grow" strategy may be taken in increments. Some firms may "go from addressing the issue at an 'own company' level, to addressing it at a stakeholder level with a focus on risk, to addressing it at a stakeholder level with a focus on growth,"[57] while others may directly move from Stage 2 to Stage 4.

MillerCoors provides an example of how water stewardship policies can mature and promote cost savings. MillerCoors uses a water strategy that focuses on collective action throughout its suppliers.[58] The drought in the US drove change, and the company designated strict efficiency goals. As a result, MillerCoors has saved $17 million, which is viewed as capital for reinvestment.[59]

Incorporating the water–food–energy Nexus, MillerCoors also recognizes that more than 90 percent of the water used comes from the agricultural sector.[60] The company, funded by the US Department of Agriculture's Natural Resources Conservation Service, developed its National Water Quality Initiative, which allows MillerCoors to engage with farmers in Texas to "plant native prairie grass in areas where runoff would otherwise deplete the soil of water."[61] Their efforts with farmers and ranchers not only improve crop yields, but also add to the conservation of water.

Quantifying the value of water

In order to gauge involvement in water stewardship practices and the business opportunities or limits associated with the water–food–energy Nexus, it is important to quantify the value of water through its full supply cost, full economic cost, and intrinsic value.

The *full supply* cost of water represents the "cost of supplying water to a user without considering the cost of the externalities resulting from the use of that water or the opportunity costs of foregoing alternative uses of that water."[62] Operation and maintenance and capital costs make up water's full supply cost, and externalities are viewed as side effects from its utilization.

The *full economic* cost of water incorporates the externalities described above. It is the sum of the full supply cost, the opportunity costs of the alternative use of a given water resource, and the side effects that others will experience as a result of water consumption.[63]

Lastly, *intrinsic value* of water must be considered when assigning the resource value. Intrinsic value includes water stewardship and sole existence of water when not accounting for its use to humans.

The demand for resources is an issue that affects economic and business growth and development. The water–food–energy Nexus is a current and serious issue that needs to be addressed and implemented into public policies, financial modeling, and stakeholder engagement. Although this section discussed the effects of growing demand on economic and business well-being, the effects of climate change were not explicitly considered. Climate change amplifies these issues and increases the need for innovation, and as time passes, it is clear that "business as usual" efforts will not be sufficient.

Climate change

Climate change is a perfect example of the absence of the kind of decision-making that a Nexus-like problem demands: with interdependent processes, you cannot take actions in one area without considering the effect on others. The drive for industrialization through the burning of fossil fuels satisfied goals for security, economic growth, mobility, growth in incomes and standards of living, and so much more. However, this came at the cost, almost from the start, of air pollution and its health impacts, which continue today, a build-up of greenhouse gases with resultant global warming, and the changes to our climate. Yogi Berra said it best: "*The future ain't what it used to be.*"[64]

Climate change is also emblematic of limits: there is both a limit to the amount of fossil fuels available and, clearly, limits to the amount of pollution and greenhouse gases we can emit into our atmosphere.

The previous section dealt with the demand for resources as a highly complicating factor in achieving continued growth. That challenge, through the complexity of the Nexus, and in a changing climate, presents what seems to be an insurmountable problem.

In this section, we will explore some of the not-so-obvious reasons that led to climate change. We will also detail some underappreciated and infrequently debated factors that make agreement on climate change mitigation so difficult. Impacts of climate change that have already occurred, as well as how these changes portend difficulties for the future, will be presented. Lastly, we will outline approaches to solutions that model the shift in thinking and collaboration needed to achieve abundance in such a complex situation. Later sections will address resiliency and adaptation to climate change.

How we got here

There is much scientific literature that explains climate change. Beyond the science, however, there are four periods in time that allowed the build-up of greenhouse gases to continue unabated or that stalled early attempts to rally consensus on mitigation. These are important to explore as they provide lessons in how we approach solutions going forward.

The first is marked by the science of greenhouse gas build-up and its impacts, which most feel we came to understand in recent history (late 20th century). Here we are not referring to reported studies by major oil companies, circa 1970s, but a 19th-century observation and warning.

> In 1896 the Swedish scientist Svante Arrhenius published a new idea. As humanity burned fossil fuels such as coal, which added carbon dioxide gas to the Earth's atmosphere, we would raise the planet's average temperature – a "greenhouse effect" . . . In the 1930s, people realized that the United States and North Atlantic region had warmed significantly during the previous half-century. Scientists supposed this was just a phase of some mild natural cycle, with unknown causes. Only one lone voice, the amateur G. S. Callendar, insisted that greenhouse warming was on the way.[65]

Given the debate we face even today on the accuracy of some climate change models and the complexity of the science, it is hard to argue that policy-makers let alone the scientific community should have acted on these findings. However, one could argue that a chance was missed to take a closer look. Society faced the impacts of air pollution from the burning of coal as early as the start of the industrial revolution. More recently, the "Great Smog" of London in 1952[66] was clearly understood to be the result of fossil fuel emissions, much the same as severe air pollution in Beijing and Delhi are understood today.

A careful reflection on the negative impacts of an understood and accepted situation (air pollution) with science that predicted other consequences could have led to more observation and perhaps earlier attempts to mitigate. The lesson is that any problem, complex or simple, is easier to solve when the scale is still small.

The second time period brings us into the 20th century when, in 1938, G.S. Callendar argued that greenhouse global warming due to CO_2 emissions from industrial activities was underway.[67] In 1956, Gil Plass calculated[68] that adding CO_2 to the atmosphere would have a significant effect on the radiation balance, and in 1957, Roger Revelle found[69] that CO_2 produced by humans will not be readily absorbed by the oceans.

These "signals" strongly link to the "precautionary principle" which states that

> if an action or policy has a suspected risk of causing harm to the public, or to the environment, in the absence of scientific consensus (that the action or policy is not harmful), the burden of proof that it is not harmful falls on those taking that action.[70]

One of the primary foundations of the precautionary principle, and globally accepted definitions, results from the work of the Rio Conference, or "Earth Summit" in 1992. The principle 15 of the Rio Declaration notes:

> In order to protect the environment, the precautionary approach shall be widely applied by States according to their capabilities. Where there are threats of serious or irreversible damage, lack of full scientific certainty shall not be used as a reason for postponing cost-effective measures to prevent environmental degradation.[71]

This is the second lesson.

The third time period started in the 1990s and extends perhaps even through the present. Here we see early attempts to rally support for action on climate change mitigation at the political level. While one could argue that such efforts were well overdue, many fell into a trap of using casual and obvious conditions in the present to explain and even offer proof of more complex scenarios. While tempting, such an approach can backfire with unintended consequences.

A common example is the need for water conservation during a drought. As a drought drags on in severity and duration, civil society, government, and others are quick to act on water conservation measures. The public and industry respond as all can see the impacts of the drought: on landscapes, reservoir levels, and the like. In most cases, little public discourse examines longer term solutions to water security. The situation fails to leverage public awareness and support for positive actions on water, to begin to address more systemic problems such as infrastructure investment needs, curbs on water allocations, water pricing, and the like. Such actions are needed pre-drought and post-drought and would also lessen the impacts of future droughts (and floods).

So, the irony of the adage comes to fruition: the worst thing that can happen during a drought is for it to rain. People's actions have been tied to the lack of rain and when it starts to rain their support for longer term action "dries up."

A good example of this casual connection in the climate change mitigation space comes from a US Senate hearing in 1988, organized by Senator Tim Wirth,[72] on global warming, leading to US involvement and negotiations in the 1992 Kyoto Summit and the eventual Kyoto Protocol. In the hot summer of 1988, Senator Wirth and his organizers checked forecasts and scheduled the hearing for an especially warm day in June.

> What we did was went in the night before and opened all the windows, I will admit, right? So that the air conditioning wasn't working inside the room and so when the, when the hearing occurred there was not only bliss, which is television cameras

in double figures, but it was really hot . . . So Hansen's giving this testimony, you've got these television cameras back
there heating up the room, and the air conditioning in the
room didn't appear to work. So it was sort of a perfect collection of events that happened that day, with the wonderful Jim
Hansen, who was wiping his brow at the witness table and giving this remarkable testimony.[73]

The casual connection here was to link the current weather (easily observed and understood) to the topic of climate change (long
term, not well-understood or observed). While apparently effective
at the time, we now see repeated counter arguments to the reality
of climate change and global warming when we face a cold, wintry
day. *The lesson here: in the long run, it does not help to make the easy argument for a hard decision* – it won't hold up over time and could come
back to bite you.

The fourth lesson is that getting others to go "all in" with you
demands that you provide a lot of evidence to convince them to
do so. A lot of evidence requires a lot of time for others to digest,
understand, debate, and make a decision.

It's hard to pin a specific date, and this shift certainly varies
across peoples, but until somewhere around the start of the 21st
century, policy-makers, governments, and the general public did
not have a "history" with greenhouse gas buildup, global warming,
and climate change. We did not study it in school, see legislation
enacted, or see consequences of climate change until the current
era. What's more, we also do not have an emotional or spiritual
connection to the topic of climate change. This is certainly changing but, from the start, our view on climate change is fundamentally
different from challenges related to water, human health, prosperity, and economic growth.

We have all had to learn about the topic together and in a relatively short amount of time. But the scientific community has
predicted that we do not have a lot of time – we must act now to
mitigate to avoid the worst of modeled and forecasted impacts.

We have been given what is to most highly scientific and complex
calculations, data, and models of predicted change. We were then

called to believe and act. These actions require huge investments, curbs on kinds of growth, fundamental changes in infrastructure and even lifestyles.

This may well all be unavoidable – we must make these changes. The mistake is not in what scientists tell us needs to be done but in their rebuttal of doubt with the same arguments as before. You quickly reach a stalemate when one asks why they should do something and the other replies "because I told you to." The obvious analogy is that we are reduced to a parent–child relationship.[74]

What we left on the table

In the absence of on authoritarian setting, you need to use all your ammunition to make the case for others to agree to big investments and big change. Yes, the science of climate change and its causes are unequivocal but most people don't understand the science. And yes, politics, business and even personal interests have clouded the climate change debate.

But all of this falls back to a single argument: believe the science and you will act; doubt it even a fraction and it's hard to make the commitment to change. As in academic debate, you win when you provide the most convincing evidence for your side. The climate change community has left a lot of evidence on the table. We are not referring to more scientific evidence but other, relatable arguments to bolster action for which the motivation threshold is much lower:

- Air pollution from fossil fuel emissions and the impact on human health and the quality life is observable, widespread, and can be quantified in economic and aesthetic terms.
- Continuity, wide availability, and renewability of alternate energy forms such as solar and wind are also observable and can be compared to finite reserves of fossil fuels in economic terms.
- The ethical and moral push (even imperative) to act with Pope Francis' recent encyclical Laudato Si'[75] provides even spiritual arguments to act, in contrast to no such arguments for continued fossil fuel use.

- Economic security, national security, and energy independence from decreased (or even eliminated) foreign sources of fossil fuels can be quantified.
- Related benefits of mitigation actions such as healthier ecosystems from reduced air and water pollution and fossil fuel extraction and refining processes can be evidenced.
- Analysis and economic benefit quantification can be made of decentralized widespread energy production from solar and wind power generation, and fewer but larger centralized power generation operations.

These arguments can stand on their own to motivate action. They can certainly be combined for greater positive impact. And, most importantly, you can debate and act on these without even introducing the topic of climate change. You can even mobilize support for such actions amongst climate skeptics, agnostics, and deniers.

We need to ask ourselves whether it is important to have everyone understand, believe, and acknowledge the science of manmade global warming and climate change as a prelude or at least in parallel with actions to mitigate. That is a tall order, perhaps the tallest. For what other topic is there complete agreement? The existence of God and the "proper" religion to worship that god? The best way to educate our children? Any "flat earthers" out there?

Impacts of climate change

There is continued debate on the relationship between climate change and the intensity, duration, and/or frequency of extreme events such as prolonged droughts in Brazil, Australia, and California, intense storms and resultant flooding and other damage, and heat waves. Certainly these events have been recorded over centuries and occur naturally. They can also be exacerbated by other actions by mankind that are independent of fossil fuel use, such as with increased and more widespread flooding from greater paved areas and the channelization of rivers, disconnecting them from natural floodplains.

But if climate change models prove accurate, such recent events can also be seen as "signals" such as those described earlier, and we can expect more such events and their resultant impacts. As such, we cannot discount these events solely because of the lack of absolute proof of climate change causation.

There are also other examples of events and observations that are predicted by climate change:

- Recurring higher-than-historical average air temperatures in southern China affecting tea cultivation.[76]
- Rising sea levels and storm/tidal surges in the Ben Tre province of Vietnam in the Mekong Delta.[77]
- Increased electrical costs for cooling due to the five-year California drought.[78]
- Decreased hydropower output from reduced water flows and reservoir levels.
- Decreased thermal power generation from the inability to extract water from rivers and/or water temperature rise.
- Lack of sufficient drinking water supplies due to drought.[79]

Potential solutions

We have already seen how missed signals, the lack of caution, casual connections, and the like can contribute to creating or magnifying a significant problem like climate change. We have also argued for using a comprehensive set of arguments that speak convincingly, collectively and individually, to the widest set of stakeholders, building momentum for contributive and collective action on a common objective but perhaps with different motivations.

But climate change is already here having real and negative impacts. What can we do? First, the lessons and approaches shown earlier can still be used to address climate change and other complex problems. There are also other, unique approaches that have shown success in addressing climate change and can be further leveraged toward real solutions.

Before describing these approaches it is important to define the nature of climate change. It is a complex problem which is the highest order of problem type, from the simple, then complicated to complex. Complex problems have ambiguous cause–effect relationships:

uncertainty, nonlinearity and feedback are inherent, and emergent properties dominate system behavior and response.

Like any problem but especially complex problems, the approach to a solution always has hallmarks such as collaboration across sectors, the long view, magnitude of change, setting bold goals, champions, and the willingness to retrench and take a new direction.

The first example starts with an activist campaign and ends with a global agreement on the phase-out of hydrofluorocarbons (HFCs). These are organic compounds commonly used as refrigerant gases but are potent greenhouse gases and, with their inadvertent or deliberate discharge to the atmosphere, are significant contributors to global warming. HFCs largely replaced refrigerant and other gaseous compounds that were gradually phased out and then banned as a result on the Montreal Protocol[80] in the late 1980s due to their negative impact on the atmosphere's ozone layer. These compounds are known as chlorofluorocarbons (CFCs) and include R-12 refrigerant gas.

At the 2002 Summer Olympic Games in Sydney, Australia, the international activist NGO Greenpeace launched a public campaign against The Coca-Cola Company entitled "Enjoy Climate Change" which employed the use of Coca-Cola's trademark script and styling, as well as the former ad tagline of "Enjoy."

Greenpeace also tugged on emotions as it played off of Coca-Cola's traditional holiday advertising motif of polar bears, showing, in cartoon, a mother bear and cubs stranded on an ice floe, presumably the result of melting polar ice sheets.

Greenpeace did not target Coca-Cola because it thought it was the biggest contributor to fugitive HFCs from its millions of vending machines and coolers around the world, though this was not to be discounted altogether. Coca-Cola was targeted, "brand-jacked" some said, as a way to gain attention to and hopeful action on the impacts of HFCs.

Coca-Cola's response is a lesson in the shift in thinking and type of action that is needed for complex problem-solving.

Then Coca-Cola CEO Doug Daft responded with two hallmarks of effective, complex problem-solving: (1) he used his position as CEO to make himself and the company a champion for the cause, and, (2) he made a bold commitment shortly after the Greenpeace campaign launched: that by the *next* Summer Olympic Games (Athens, Greece in 2004), the company would work to develop commercially viable alternatives to CFCs for as refrigerant gases and begin their use. The company would later set goals to use only non-HFC refrigerant solutions as older equipment was phased out and new equipment was introduced. The ultimate objective for the company is to be HFC-free.[81]

In working to progress towards this goal, Coca-Cola demonstrated two other hallmarks needed for complex problem-solving:

(1) Instead of rebutting, condemning, or ignoring Greenpeace, Coca-Cola proactively engaged with them to explore solutions. This did not mean they became partners but they did form a relationship of mutual respect and the desire to contribute to progress versus continued animosity, played out in the media.

(2) Coca-Cola realized that though its scale of coolers and as a result HFC gases was large, it could not solve the problem alone. The company saw that to achieve the research needed and commercialization of business scale, cost-effective solutions from the global supply chain in refrigerant gases and cooler manufacturers, it would need several more companies and organizations to get on board. Coca-Cola appreciated that sometimes to solve a company problem you have to change the industry. This resulted in the eventual formation of "Refrigerants Naturally,"[82] whose tagline is "Clever Cooling Versus Global Warming." This diverse set of actors, supported by Greenpeace, is allowing Coca-Cola, and many others, to progress toward an HFC-free future.

In October of 2016, in Kigali, Rwanda, some 150 nations gathered to adopt a global resolution[83] to phase out HFCs, with specific targets and timetables, trade sanction options for countries that fall behind, and financial aid for developing-world nations.

Another, more recent example of a champion setting a bold goal is Walmart's "Project Gigaton."[84] Announced at its Bentonville, Arkansas, headquarters on April 19, 2017, while flanked by leading conservation NGOs such as WWF and the Nature Conservancy, Walmart "asks suppliers to reduce greenhouse gas emissions by one gigaton – the equivalent to taking more than 211 million passenger vehicles off of US roads for an entire year" by 2030. In addition to being a bold goal-setter and champion, Walmart also makes use of important leverage points to collective problem-solving: its large buying power can drive supplier action and its large presence gives a big voice to the debate and action.

A third example employs the long view toward complex problem-solving and collaboration across sectors. It also employs powerful approaches of welcoming disparate views and framing the problem outside the context of most debates. In 2014, under the leadership of Secretary Ernest Moniz, the US Department of Energy (DOE) launched a report on the nexus of water and energy.[85] This report took both sides of the long view: (1) the research and debate contributing to the report spanned several years and harvested data from much earlier, and (2) the findings and recommendations were not only intended for present-day policy responses, but to survive changes in administration for the road ahead.

In collecting and discussing data, challenges, and solutions the DOE engaged a wide collection of leading voices from business, academia, research, other government functions, industry, civil society, and communities. In doing so, the DOE deliberately invited those with counter arguments *against* change. Secretary Moniz realized that the tough choices and investments needed for complex problem-solving would not easily be achieved if the "no vote" was systematically shut out or shouted down from the start.

The DOE also took advantage of leaving nothing on the table, but with a twist. The process and report looked at all manner of data, policy, decision-making, and available choices to build sound conclusions and recommendations, not relying on any one factor or data set to predominate the debate. The twist was, in the opinion of author G. Koch (who was part of the development process with the DOE), the deliberate downplay, sometimes even absence, of the impacts of climate change in discussing water–energy nexus changes and challenges. Secretary Moniz easily recognized the charged, political atmosphere, both in Washington D.C. and beyond, that came with climate change debate. He also saw that he didn't need it. Yes, climate change was a major wrench in the works, a force multiplier bringing uncertainty, but he and his staff saw they could make more progress on what most (sometimes all) engaged could agree on by framing the problem *without* climate change.

Notes

1 Swaminathan, M. S., *Combating Hunger and Achieving Food Security*, Cambridge University Press, 2016.
2 World Business Council on Sustainable Development (WBCSD), *Co-Optimizing Solutions: Water and Energy for Food, Feed and Fiber*, October 2015.
3 Ibid.
4 Sarni, *Deflecting the Scarcity Trajectory: Innovation at the Water, Energy, and Food Nexus*, Deloitte University Press, 2015.
5 Ibid.
6 Ibid.
7 Ibid.
8 Ibid.
9 Ibid.
10 Ibid.
11 Ibid.
12 Hardin, G. "The Tragedy of the Commons," *Science* 162 (3859): 1243–1248. doi:10.1126/science.162.3859.1243. PMID 5699198, 1968.
13 Nexus, "The Water, Energy and Food Security Nexus – Bonn2011 Nexus Conference," https://www.water-energy-food.org/calendar/detail/2012-02-27-conference-the-water-energy-and-food-security-nexus-bonn2011-nexus-conference/, accessed September 29, 2017.
14 Ibid.
15 Cate Lamb, "How Should Business React to China's Water Crisis?" *World Economic Forum*, July 21, 2016.
16 Lloyd's, "Global Water Scarcity Risks and Challenges for Business," *Handbook of Water Economics*, WWF, 2010.
17 Ibid.
18 Ibid.
19 Ibid.
20 Ibid.
21 Ibid.
22 Ibid.
23 Ibid.
24 Ibid.
25 Ibid.
26 Ibid.
27 Ibid.

28 Ibid.
29 Ibid.
30 Sarni, *Getting Ahead of the "Ripple Effect:" A Framework for a Water Stewardship Strategy*, Deloitte University Press, January 31, 2013.
31 Ibid.
32 Ibid.
33 Ibid.
34 Ibid.
35 Ibid.
36 Ibid.
37 Ibid.
38 Ibid.
39 Ibid.
40 Ibid.
41 Ibid.
42 Ibid.
43 Ibid.
44 Ibid.
45 Ibid.
46 Ibid.
47 Will Sarni, *Fueling Growth: You Can't Always Buy What You Need*, Deloitte University Press, 2014.
48 Ibid.
49 Ibid.
50 Ibid.
51 Ibid.
52 Ibid.
53 Ibid.
54 Ibid.
55 Ibid.
56 Ibid.
57 Ibid.
58 Ibid.
59 Ibid.
60 Ibid.
61 Ibid.
62 Ibid.
63 Ibid.
64 Berra, Yogi, https://www.brainyquote.com/quotes/quotes/y/yogiberra102747.html, accessed November 20, 2017.
65 Ibid.
66 Texas A&M, "Researchers Solve Mystery of Historic 1952 London Fog And Current Chinese Haze," November 14, 2016.
67 Weart, Spencer R., *The Discovery of Global Warming*, Harvard University Press, 2008.
68 Ibid.
69 Ibid.

70 Timothy O'Riordon, *Interpreting the Precautionary Principle*, Routledge, 2013.

71 UNEP, Declaration on Environment and Development, Principle 15, Rio, 1992.

72 PBS *Frontline*, Hot Interviews: Timothy Wirth, January 17, 2007.

73 Ibid.

74 Joe Concha, "The Death of Civil Discourse: Twitterverse Eviscerates Bret Stephens Over Climate Column," *The Hill*, April 30, 2017.

75 Pope Francis, "Laudato Si'," June 18, 2015.

76 Author's observations and WWF.

77 Ibid.

78 Brooke Ruth and Maureen Cavanaugh, "Report: California's Five-Year Drought Increased Electricity Costs By $2.45B," KPBS, April 26, 2017.

79 Pacific Institute, *Drought and Equity in California*, January 2017.

80 UNEP, "The Montreal Protocol on Substances that Deplete the Ozone Layer," September 16, 1987.

81 Coca-Cola Company, *Climate Protection Report*, www.coca-colacompany.com/climate-protection-report, accessed Sept. 19, 2017.

82 "Clever Cooling vs. Global Warming," RefrigerantsNaturally.com homepage, www.refrigerantsnaturally.com/, accessed September 19, 2017.

83 Coral Davenport, "Nations, Fighting Powerful Refrigerant That Warms Planet, Reach Landmark Deal," *New York Times*, October 15, 2016.

84 Walmart, "Walmart Launches Project Gigaton to Reduce Emissions in Company's Supply Chain," April 19, 2017.

85 US Department of Energy, Office of the Undersecretary for Science and Energy, "The Water-Energy Nexus: Challenges and Opportunities," accessed September 19, 2017.

3

TOUGH CHOICES – THE TRADEOFFS

Adulthood requires one take on responsibility, not only for one's self but most often for others, whether in a family or work environment. This shift from a relatively carefree life of a young child to maturity is gradual, with important milestones of schooling, training, marriage, promotion to management at work, raising children, and so on. As Angela Scott Moore wrote "Now you understand why Peter Pan didn't want to grow up."[1]

Increasing levels of responsibility with greater costs and consequences of decision-making face the policymaker and corporate executive alike.

Sometimes, throughout all journeys of leadership, a complicated, even complex, problem will arise and its solution often involves tradeoffs that come from a tough decision being made: the proverbial "win–win" solution becomes more difficult to find and achieve as the magnitude and interlinkages of various problem sets increase.

As we have detailed the challenges before us all in the previous chapters, we now turn to the subject of tough decisions by first explaining why tough decisions are so hard to make.

We will look at previous tradeoffs and tough decisions from history and further outline the key tradeoffs we need to make as we seek well-being and abundance. This chapter ends with recommendations to make such difficult choices more acceptable by those affected.

Why is it hard to make tough decisions?

Tough decisions most often involve a tradeoff with one entity (or several) not getting what they seek or being forced to accept only some portion of their objective. The person in a position of authority making that decision will face consequences.

A parent could face sad children that tug at their heart strings. A manager could face disgruntled workers leading to low morale and decreased productivity in the office. A politician could upset a large bloc of unhappy voters in the next election. There is even guilt often faced by the winning party who sees the impact on those who did not get what they wanted. A good example of this in the workplace is employees who survive a downsizing and keep their jobs while feeling remorse, even guilt, seeing friends and co-workers laid off.

This factor of personal ill feeling by the one who decides and those who are affected is common in the aftermath of most tough decisions. And, while the desire to avoid such feelings can be a strong roadblock to decision-making, there are other factors that influence the process of reaching an ultimate decision.

One such factor is well known in the financial world: short-term thinking. Daily fluctuations and stock market prices and quarterly earnings reported by corporations often influence decisions by senior managers and corporate boards. While it is important to pay attention to and understand the reaction of financial markets, most corporations make and execute plans for the medium and long term and should not pay heed to daily and weekly fluctuations.

Short-term thinking can certainly effect the decisions made by a politician who faces an imminent re-election as well as the parent who opts for a night of relative peace and quiet in deciding to let her children stay up past their bedtime. We live in the here and now and the pervasiveness of information at our fingertips through the Internet, smart phones and social media only serves to reinforce short-term thinking and actions.

Another example of short-term thinking is over-reliance on the immediate past. We see this in many places after rains begin, ending a long drought, such as the recent five-year one in California.[2] The conservation efforts and cooperation on long-term plans to reduce vulnerability and increase resiliency for future droughts often "dries up," reinforcing the adage the "worst thing that happens in a drought is for the rain to start." However, some promising trends suggest we have learned from our past mistakes, with Californians vowing to maintain conservation efforts.[3]

Such confidence in the recent past is being upended with the effects of climate change. A case in point is the Colorado River Compact,[4] signed in 1922, which is an agreement between the seven western states in the US to allocate available water. Though court battles and debate have occurred almost since the signing, the majority of such discussions centered on how much each state should receive, with a continued reliance on the historic and projected flows as the basis for such allocation. Recent studies indicate[5] that the 1922 allocations and projections, with amendments since, were based on a relatively wet period for the Colorado River drainage basin and the future might see much less water to meet increasing demands.

To illustrate this point, author Koch recently visited an industrial manufacturing facility in India where he noted the apparent young average age of the workforce. The plant manager, whose mandate is to innovate across all aspects of production, stated that he purposely sought young, inexperienced workers who "were not saddled with the baggage of experience." That is, he didn't want experienced workers from other facilities who might resist new ways of working, citing they had "always done it that way" without questioning.

Conversely, there is a tendency *not* to rely enough on the historic past. History is replete with examples of peoples and governments who made decisions leading to significant negative consequences and even their downfall.

Jared Diamond's *Collapse: How Societies Choose to Fail or Succeed*[6] provides excellent examples of decisions, tough or otherwise, that were not made well, from Scandinavia's failure to adapt to the local situation in attempting to settle Greenland, to the different choices on natural resource management between Haiti and the Dominican Republic on the island of Hispaniola, the impact of which can be graphically seen today.

Another factor making decisions difficult in a complicated or complex situation is information. Yes, through the Internet we have an abundance of information, but this can be overwhelming to absorb and rife with opposing views. On the flip side is the lack of information one faces when you consider the confidentiality (or lack of transparency) of much information needed to make complex decisions. For example, in California, which recently passed legislation seeking to sustainably manage its groundwater resources,[7] regulators face a dearth of information on existing water abstraction from many farmers and irrigators reluctant to report data, fearing rising costs and limits on groundwater use from such regulation.

Since most of the challenges, and therefore solutions, presented herein involve water, it is important to point out some unique characteristics of decision-making for water. These are best summed by Peter Gleick who once stated "water is not rocket science, its harder."[8] It is harder because of the spiritual, even religious, connection we have to water. It is harder because everyone and everything needs water, and therefore, solutions need to take *all* viewpoints into account. Since it moves though societies, economies, and ecosystem so profoundly, it requires policymakers to reach across the aisle and across agencies and ministries. Finally, though not unique to water, corruption is a major challenge and factor in tough decision-making. Transparency International cites high levels of corruption, across many geographies, in large-scale water infrastructure constructions projects such as dams, water treatment plants, and sewage and drainage systems.[9]

A final factor that challenges tough decision-making involves how we interpret new information. Interconnected challenges, their project impacts and possible solutions will often involve new data and information being presented that requires understanding. A good example is global warming and climate change. The underlying data and models are complicated and extensive. These data need to be seen, learned, and applied to what one currently thinks of the climate (which is very little, for most of us) in order for perceptions to change and, hence, acceptance for the costs of proposed solutions to be accepted. Professor Dave Snowden with the consultancy Cognitive Edge[10] has researched decision-making in complex environments extensively and has shown how the majority of people review new data and information with only a partial scan, relying on this incomplete knowledge and their past experiences to make decisions or form opinions.

An excellent case study Snowdon cites involves radiologists viewing multiple x-rays of patient lungs to determine the presence of cancerous nodules.[11] Eight-three percent of the radiologists in the study failed to see the image of a gorilla the size of a matchbook superimposed on the x-rays.

We see what we expect to see, and this is a major challenge in reaching consensus, or at least acceptance, on tough decisions.

Difficult decisions from the past and their consequences

There are certainly many tough decisions with tradeoffs before us all. Chief among them is perhaps slowing, stopping, and possibly reversing global warming and the impacts of climate change. Even if we fail at these and choose (or are forced) to adapt, the choices we will need to make in reducing vulnerability and increasing resiliency will be difficult in their own right. Odds are that we will need to do both: make difficult choices to combat it, and adapt to live with climate change.

In the last section of this chapter, as well as the remainder of the book, we will posit potential solutions.

There are many decisions made in the past with significant, negative consequences. One can look at many of these as having been made in the absence of sufficient information or thorough analyses of possible consequences. Some may also have been made by a despot intent on wrongdoing. Others may suffer from the lack of scientific knowledge or access to ready information and the lines of communications we enjoy today. Hindsight is often 20–20, as they say, but let us refer to these as "mistakes."

What we will look at here, to learn from, are a handful of tough decisions from history that can be viewed as having enough knowledge and information in the context of when they were made.

The first example is the British evacuation of their troops from Dunkirk, France, in the late spring of 1940, during World War II.[12] Nearly 350,000 allied troops were evacuated versus staying to fight the advancing German army, which subsequently occupied all of continental Europe across the English Channel, including Belgium, France, and the Netherlands. What's more, Britain now faced the prospect of invasion and many thought the British government would sue for peace with Germans.

The outcome of World War II is known and there are many factors including over-extension of German forces on two fronts (West and East into Russia) and the role of the United States that led to victory for the allies. But it is clear that the tough decision to accept temporary defeat, face criticism, and diminish the confidence of the British armed forces and its generals was the correct decision, as it preserved the lives of the fighting force needed in future battle.

The lessons include losing a battle to win a war and accepting short-term humiliation for longer term glory.

The second decision also involves the British. During World War II, 730 representatives of 44 governments met during July of 1944 at the Mount Washington Hotel in Bretton Woods, New Hampshire. Bretton Woods Conference, formally known as the United Nations Monetary and Financial Conference, was aimed at alleviating the human and economic misery resulting from the War, allow for growth and reconstruction through the establishment commercial and financial processes to allow for robust trade, through increased lending, and economic stability. "The Bretton Woods system was the first example of a fully-negotiated monetary order intended to govern monetary relations among independent nation-states."[13]

The agreement signed at the end of the conference gave rise to the International Monetary Fund (IMF) and the International Bank for Reconstruction and Development (IBRD), which today, with the World Bank, are part of the World Bank Group.

> The chief features of the Bretton Woods system were an obligation for each country to adopt a monetary policy that maintained the exchange rate ($\pm 1\%$) by tying its currency to gold and the ability of the IMF to bridge temporary imbalances of payments.[14] Also, there was a need to address the lack of cooperation among other countries and to prevent competitive devaluation of the currencies as well.[15]

The United States successfully argued that the US dollar (then backed by gold) or gold would be the only acceptable reserves for all to rely on. In agreeing to the US dollar, the British relinquished supremacy of the pound sterling and thereby its ability control trade on its terms, especially with its widespread colonies.

But Britain had many debts to pay from World War II, especially to the US. It had a country to rebuild and an economy to grow, and so ratified the agreement. The lesson is to swallow pride and historical feelings of privilege, and allow a political and economic adversary to prevail.

President John F. Kennedy and the Cuban Missile Crisis of 1962 offer the lesson of faith in mankind.[16] Spy photography by the US confirmed the Soviet Union was installing nuclear missiles in Cuba, some 100 miles from the US mainland. Much diplomatic and political debate ensued by the end of the crisis. The Soviet withdrawal of the missiles from Cuba came after President Kennedy ordered a naval blockade of Cuba, preventing further offensive weapons or other material to enter or leave Cuba. There are certainly many factors leading to the Soviet decision to withdraw, and much scholarly literature analyzes the incident, its causes, and aftermath. However, it is the authors' opinion that a large part of President Kennedy's decision was the faith that the Soviets would not risk nuclear war and possible mutual destruction with the US. That is, in dire situations, mutual respect and moral principle can aid in decision-making.

The last example is the creation and the enactment into law of the National Environmental Protection Act (NEPA) in the US. In June 1972, the Technical Analysis Division (TAD) of the US National Bureau of Standards prepared a retrospective study, sponsored by the Environmental Protection Agency (EPA), on the events, debate, and eventual creation of NEPA. NEPA is important to understand, as it required government projects to undergo environmental impact assessments (EIAs) and was the precursor to the creation of the EPA Clean Air Act and the Clean Water Act.

In its 1973 report,[17] TAD notes that the

issues involved were quite complex. And, in order to set NEPA in the proper context, TAD found it useful to describe (1) the rapid growth of an environmental ethic in the US,

(2) the impact of some highly visible ecological disasters which captured national attention, and (3) the traditional maneuvering and in-fighting characteristic of the American political system.

The study offers valuable lessons, including:

- Activist organizations should not be marginalized or ignored as they may well point to problems at a stage when their solution is easier to obtain.
- A well-informed public, and responsible media, given time can greatly influence political action.
- Seemingly herculean tasks with tremendously high projected costs can be achieved once the political will and agreement are achieved (for example the significant improvement in water and air quality the US achieved since the 1970s, without economic ruin or stagnation due to the costs).
- Once achieved, sustained improvements yield benefits and abundance for the long term (think of the growth in communities and economies, as well as improvements in public health and the personal and economic growth that ensued, due to cleaner water and air).

The choices we face

Before facing tough decisions, it is important, in the context of the challenges presented herein, to accept that the choices must be made. If we are to continue to grow, prosper, achieve well-being, even have abundance, we must make choices to enable this. As Figure 3.1 illustrates, throughout human history, with the advent of some new technology, improved means of organization, or awareness from new observations and knowledge, peoples and later governments and organizations have made the tough decision to change direction.

Some took such decisions early while others lagged, some have not fully transitioned to the new status or realized the full potential of the change, but in each case, a decision was made. Many decisions happen over time and many are not made by any one actor, but rather by society. And, yes, some decisions involve investing significant resources and required wholescale shifts in society.

As illustrated in Figure 3.1, one can debate the timing of the events shown, as well as lobby for other discoveries or events that lead to similar change, but it is clear that: (1) there are peoples, companies, societies, and nations that have not yet made a given change. In fact, there exist today hunter-gatherer communities, basic agrarian societies, and all manner of variations across the spectrum of development; and (2) for any given people or organization, if they have not made the change or are late to making the decision to progress, it will be harder — sometimes impossible — to progress further. There are many examples of conquered people, bankrupt corporations, and failed nation states where the ultimate reason for failure is the lack of decision.

The lack of decision may not be due to inaction. For example, there are many times when a culture that dominates in some way (such as with military weaponry or by means of communication) was able to conquer another who had not yet made or acquired such discoveries. Jared Diamond in *Guns, Germs and Steel: The Fate of Human Societies*[19] provides several convincing examples of history illustrating such dominance.

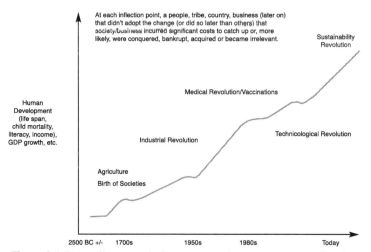

Failure Due to Lack of Decision

Figure 3.1 **Key milestones in human development and implications to societies**

Source: Adapted from Diamond, 1999.[18]

However, the challenges we face today in a modern world cannot be said to lack information, means of communication, and resources to understand our dilemma and act.

The tough decisions we all need to make involve:

- Facing limits on growth in some sectors and in some geographies: an example is the decline in Saudi Arabia's agriculture production, which has mostly depleted its groundwater reserves, leading to higher costs to import food and to enter into long-term contracts of land in other countries dedicated to produce food destined for export to the Kingdom.[20]
- Paying higher upfront and recurring costs for some goods and services: many Californians face higher water service fees or other forms of taxation to recover and maintain costs with desalination systems installed to alleviate pressure on freshwater supplies.[21]
- Being more willing to relocate and more accommodating of those that migrate to your region: corn cultivation is increasing in Canada due to the shift in climate bringing warmer temperatures.[22]
- Accepting and managing uncertainty: volatility in commodity prices due to more frequent and unpredictable weather extremes.[23]

How to ease the pain?

If one accepts not only the challenges presented herein but also the urgency of action that is needed, we first offer a recommendation on what is *not* needed – more data and newer technology.

This is not to say that more accurate and comprehensive information and its timely update is not welcome, nor that some problems do require additional research. It also does *not* mean that innovative technologies or the novel application of existing technology is not useful, perhaps even necessary, in the longer term.

We argue here against the tendency to use the lack of complete data or the absence of some breakthrough discovery just over the horizon as an excuse for inaction today. At a minimum, action needs to progress through difficult decision-making *today* while advancing knowledge gaps. In doing so, it is important to leave room for adjustment in policy, treaties, and other decisions, to allow for flexibility as more becomes known.

Another important factor to realize is human psychology and our response to change – the human stress response.[24] The classic response consists of either fight (resist the change or "shoot the messenger"), flight (ignore the new information, avoid debate and further learning), freeze (shut down), or please (readily accept change without thoughtful consideration of options and consequences).

As many of the changes from tough decisions that need to be made will induce stress among the many, policymakers and decision-makers would be wise to understand and accept these responses and allow for time for more people to reach understanding and be open to debate.

Chapter 5 will provide our thoughts on the way forward, but it is clear that to make the changes required, we will certainly need vocal champions across society. We will also need selfless leaders with courage. Incentives and penalties, whether market driven or through regulation, can also play an important role. Beyond these more obvious characteristics, we offer three approaches to help the decision-making process more effective and with a higher likelihood of success:

1   Principled pragmatism: Professor Shafiqul Islam of Tufts University advocates for this approach in the context of water diplomacy (or negotiations).[25] As we have shown, many of the tough decisions before us include water, so this approach may well have widespread applicability.

Islam rightly points out that

> complex problems are connected with many competing and often conflicting values, interests, and tools. These problems can't be addressed through simply applying dogmatic principles or a deal-making, purely pragmatic approach . . . Any intervention to a complex problem requires attention to both principles and pragmatism. Strict adherence to principles without pragmatism is often not actionable; pure pragmatism exercised without guiding principles is not sustainable.[26]

If, for example, we accept the desired longevity of a given water source – its sustainability – and equity in its use as principles, the debate toward a solution can be focused on practices and their changes, always grounded in the shared values of these principles.

2   The right components of good policy: a well-written set of rules is a start but the fulfilment of its objectives requires more. Three aspects of effective policy are required: the right level of authority, sufficient capacity to implement and enforce regulations, and adequate funding. The absence or insufficiency of any one of these will undermine the overall policy.

Take the US Senator Paul Simon *Water for the World Act* which

[e]xpresses the sense of Congress that: (1) water and sanitation are critically important resources that impact many aspects of human life, and (2) the United States should be a global leader in helping provide sustainable access to clean water and sanitation for the world's most vulnerable populations.[27]

As a US Congress bill signed into law by the president, it could have no higher level of authority. The United States Agency for International Development (USAID), an arm of the US Department of State, is the main organization tasked with helping developing world communities and governments implement access to safe drinking water, sanitation, and hygiene (WASH). In their report for the fiscal year ending June 30, 2015, USAID reports that, "as of 2015, more than 7.6 million people have received improved access to drinking water supply; more than 4.3 million people have received improved access to sanitation facilities."[28] This is clear demonstration that USAID has the capacity to deliver. However, funding for USAID and their programs is subject to annual appropriations by Congress and approval by the president. However, though "since 2008, USAID has allocated more than $2.9 billion on WASH and has continually worked to increase the effectiveness and sustainability of that programming,"[29] future appropriations may decrease and limit their ability to achieve longer term goals.[30]

Another example comes from Koch's meeting with a West African nation's minister of water in 2005. Asked what was hindering progress on increased access to improved sources of water, the minister stated that he had the proper level of authority and that funding (foreign assistance and domestic reserves) was adequate for the goals established at the time. He cited insufficient capacity of regulators trained in the topic and insufficient local supplies and services (such a groundwater well drillers) to allow for cost-effective execution.

3   "Money talks," so the saying goes. Tough decisions most often require significant investment and/or will lead to economic impact in the future. As such, an economic analysis and presentation of the problem can be a powerful approach to reaching consensus. In the case of water, economic valuation presents a convincing frame and motivator for positive action toward sustainable solutions.

One example is the valuation of water services from the perspective of public infrastructure, to deliver safe drinking water and provide sanitation. The initial provision and upkeep of infrastructure to provide and sustain water and sanitation can benefit from a pragmatic measure of market valuation, one distinguishing between water as a *substance* and water *services*.

If you speak only of water the *substance* you conflate the substance with the *service*. This conflation makes discussions on how to fund necessary infrastructure almost impossible. How can you charge for something that falls from the sky? And, yes, societies *can* decide that its provision in a form available and suitable for drinking is also a right. However, that does not excuse a society from investing the capital and running costs to capture, store, treat, and distribute water. These are economic goods that do cost money (labor, infrastructure, chemicals, and energy). We do not mean to say that these should not be provided to the poor at reasonable costs or even free, subsidized by others in society. It does mean that you need to separate the discussion of the substance from the service.

We pay so much for other services without ever thinking of the substance. What do you pay for when you buy electricity, or gasoline, or cellular services? Electrons, fuel, or bars on your phone? No, you buy security/warmth/convenience, mobility, and connectivity. Here, it's the service we understand and value – this same model needs to happen with water.

Similarly, the market valuation of ecosystem services is powerful, to justify and motivate watershed protection measures, with such healthy watersheds providing the supplies of water for people, such as in water funds.[31]

Finally, a hydro-economic analysis across the Nexus of food, water, and energy security has proven to be a transformative basis for government action and policy changes. This approach will be discussed in Chapter 4.

Notes

1 Angela Scott Moore, "About," https://lifegetsbetter.net/about/, accessed September 19, 2017.

2 US Geologic Survey, "California Drought Monitor," https://ca.water.usgs.gov/data/drought/, accessed September 19, 2017.

3 Jessica Mendoza, "As Historic Drought Ends, Californians Vow to Retain Water-Saving Habits," *The Christian Science Monitor*, April 18, 2017.

4 US Department of the Interior, Bureau of Reclamation, "The Law of the River," https://www.usbr.gov/lc/region/g1000/lawofrvr.html, accessed September 19, 2017.

5 David Owen, "Where the River Runs Dry," *The New Yorker*, May 25, 2015.

6 Jared Diamond, *Collapse*, Penguin Books, 2011.

7 California Department of Water Resources, Groundwater Information Center, "Key Legislation," www.water.ca.gov/groundwater/groundwater_management/legislation.cfm, accessed September 19, 2017.

8 Ramin Skibba, "Peter Gleick: Top Water Scientist Doggedly Pursues Conservation," *Out of the Fog*, April 14, 2016.

9 Transparency International, "Global Corruption Report 2008: Corruption in the Water Sector," June 2008.

10 "Home Page," Cognitive Edge, https://cognitive-edge.com/, accessed September 19, 2017.

11 Alix Spiegel, "Why Even Radiologists Can Miss A Gorilla Hiding In Plain Sight," *NPR*, February 11, 2013.

12 Encyclopedia Britannica, "Dunkirk Evacuation," https://www.britannica.com/event/Dunkirk-evacuation, accessed September 19, 2017.

13 Federal Reserve History, "Creation of the Bretton Woods System," https://www.federalreservehistory.org/essays/bretton_woods_created, accessed September 19, 2017.

14 Ibid.

15 Ibid.

16 Jutta Weldes, *Constructing National Interests: The United States and the Cuban Missile Crisis*, University of Minnesota Press, 1999.

17 Lynn G. Llewellyn and Clare Peiser, "NEPA and the Environmental Movement: A Brief History," National Bureau of Standards, Institute for Applied Technology, July 1973.

18 Jared Diamond, *Guns, Germs, and Steel: The Fates of Human Societies*, W.W. Norton & Company Inc., 1999.

19 Ibid.

20 Javier Blas, "Saudi Wells Running Dry – of Water – Spell End of Desert Wheat," Bloomberg, November 3, 2015.

21 David Gorn, "Desalination's Future in California Is Clouded by Cost and Controversy," KQED Science, October 31, 2016.

22 Alan Bjerga, "Canada's Climate Warms to Corn as Grain Belt Shifts North," Bloomberg, April 15, 2014.

23 "Sustainability and Climate Change," PWC UK, www.pwc.co.uk/services/sustainability-climate-change/insights/international-threats-and-opportunities-of-climate-change-to-the-uk.html, accessed September 19, 2017.

24 Sandra L. Bloom and Brian Farragher, *Destroying Sanctuary: The Crisis in Human Service Delivery Systems*, Oxford University Press, 2010.

25 Shafiqul Islam, "Is Principled Pragmatism a Viable Framework for Addressing Complex Problems?" Water Diplomacy, March 12, 2017.

26 Ibid.

27 Full text, "H.R.2901 – Senator Paul Simon Water for the World Act of 2014," 113th Congress.

28 USAID, "Safeguarding the World's Water: Report of Water Sector Activities," USAID, 2015.

29 Ibid.

30 Bryant Harris, Robbie Gramer, and Emily Tamkin, "The End of Foreign Aid As We Know It," *Foreign Policy*, April 24, 2017.

31 "Water Funds: Investing in Nature and Clean Water," The Nature Conservancy, https://www.nature.org/ourinitiatives/habitats/riverslakes/water-funds-investing-in-nature-and-clean-water-1.xml, accessed September 19, 2017.

4

THE OPPORTUNITIES

Resource scarcity creates opportunities. Or, as Albert Einstein put it, "In the middle of difficulty lies opportunity."[1] There are several examples of public and private sector opportunities created in response to resource scarcity and Nexus stress. For example, the recent experience of Ireland and the creation of Irish Water. The Irish Water Utility was created for a number of reasons.

Irish water infrastructure was in need of a major upgrade due to leakage and the potential for contamination. For example, in 2015, Ireland had 121 drinking water treatment plants which supplied 940,000 people, but up to 49 percent of all drinking water was lost before it reached taps. Furthermore, at least 180,000 properties were at risk of not meeting the European Union (EU) guidelines for the levels of lead in drinking water. The creation of a utility would therefore enable a standardized approach to capital investment, looking at the system as a whole as opposed to individual pieces with subsequent economies of scale.

In addition to the need to upgrade aging infrastructure the Irish water system was managed by 31 different local authorities, which resulted in duplication and inconsistencies in investments, operations, and maintenance. In contrast, by 2021, Ireland plans to invest about 5.5 billion euros in water infrastructure and services. By creating a standalone entity, the organization would be capable of borrowing money outside the government debt, which has been cited as a key reason for the establishment of the utility.

Establishing Irish Water provides Ireland with a national-owned utility with a mission to address previous challenges and ensure that all "customers receive a safe and reliable supply of drinking water and have their wastewater collected and safely returned to the environment." Irish Water "will protect the environment in all our activities and support Ireland's social and economic growth through appropriate investment in Water Services."

The utility plans to accomplish this mission through nine over-arching deliverables:

1 Establish the highest health and safety standards;
2 Implement a 5.5 billion euro capital investment program;
3 Deliver capital efficiency savings of 500 million euros;
4 Evolve Irish Water into a high-performing utility;
5 Transform the water services operating model;
6 Deliver operating cost savings of 1.1 billion euros;
7 Achieve best-practice customer service;
8 Put Irish Water on a solid commercial footing;
9 Support economic growth in line with economic and spatial planning policy.

By 2021, the utility aims to eliminate the current risk of water con-tamination, reduce leakage in the water network by 10 percent, prevent wastewater discharge without treatment, and improve water and wastewater capacity.

While Irish Water is a significant step forward for Ireland, there have been challenges. The primary challenge for Irish Water is that now consumers and customers now have to pay for water use. Unlike most countries in Europe, Ireland has not historically charged for water services, and unsurprisingly, the average amount of fresh water used for households and businesses is higher than in other countries. Once charges were imposed, less than half of the 1.5 million homes connected to Irish Water ended up complying with the charges. As a result, debts have mounted for the company as customers have refused to pay their bills.

Complicating the matter is a decision by the European Commission saying that Ireland must continue charging for water, or it will be subject to fines for non-compliance with the EU water directive. Furthermore, a recent report shows that the Irish govern-ment is able to borrow money at a cheaper rate than Irish Water. The report also questions the ability of the utility to be a standalone entity which falls outside the government debt (one of the primary reasons for establishing the utility in the first place). The EU may consider the utility overly reliant on the government for financing and therefore classify its borrowings as part of the national debt.

During April 2017, the Irish Water Committee approved Ireland's new water strategy, which eliminated water charges and refunds money to those who have already paid. The Committee had previously recommended that domestic water charging assigned under the Water Services Act of 2014 be discontinued. This will be replaced by a general taxation so households will continue to pay for water. The Committee did recommend that all new homes be fitted with water meters to ensure that water use is quantified and to develop incentives for water conservation. The working report also proposed that "those who willfully abuse water or permit wastage can be prosecuted." Excessive use of water will be set at 1.7 times the average household consumption level. This is also intended to demonstrate that Ireland is fulfilling its responsibilities under the current EU water directives.

One of the many lessons from Ireland is that consumers usually balk at paying for water, and public policy often fails to address the need for conservation and sensible pricing.

The 2030 Water Resources Group

In 2007, the Global Agenda Council (now called Global Future Councils) on Water Security of the World Economic Forum (WEF) discussed water challenges with an eye toward ultimate solutions for some of the more pressing problems. It identified water policy as the crux of long-term solutions, given both the scale and widespread interconnectedness of water within a country or other large-scale jurisdiction. Yet it realized it needed a new angle, as policy reform had been and was being attempted in many places, but with little success, considering the urgency of predicted water crises. Little success is probably best explained by Jean-Claude Juncker's famous quote about politicians facing tough choices: "We all know what to do, we just don't know how to get re-elected after we've done it."[2]

The remains of this chapter detail how those early discussions led to a groundbreaking approach to water analysis and government engagement and, ultimately, to the creation of the 2030

Water Resources Group (2030 WRG). We will then outline the growth and maturity of the organization.

The chapter ends with several examples by multi-stakeholder platforms at country level and mega-state level catalyzed and counseled by 2030 WRG (note that The Coca-Cola Company and Greg Koch are members and supporters of 2030 WRG). These will be shown as a testament to 2030 WRG's work but also as guidance for what can be achieved through similar approaches, and most importantly, to demonstrate that well-being and abundance are achievable, at reasonable cost and timeframes, if the right actors agree to work together, weigh tradeoffs, and commit to action.

Origins

Following those discussions in 2007, a group of Agenda Council member organizations and others joined together to advance the concept. These pioneers were:

- International Finance Corporation (IFC)
- McKinsey & Company (who also led research and report development)
- The Barilla Group, a global food group
- The Coca-Cola Company, a global beverage company
- Nestlé S.A., a global nutrition, health, and wellness company
- SABMiller plc, a global brewer
- New Holland Agriculture, a global agricultural equipment company
- Standard Chartered Bank, a global financial institution
- Syngenta AG, a global agribusiness

In addition to this group of sponsors and collaborators, an advisory panel was formed consisting of some of the leading minds in the water arena:

- Pasquale Steduto, Service Chief, Food and Agricultural Organization, Land and Water Unit (FAO)
- Michael Norton, Managing Director, Water and Power Group, Halcrow Group Ltd

- John Briscoe, Gordon McKay Professor of the Practice of Environmental Engineering, Harvard University
- Mark Rosegrant, Director of the Environment and Production Technology Division, International Food Policy Research Institute (IFPRI)
- Colin Chartres, Director General, International Water Management Institute (IWMI)
- Peter Börkey and Roberto Martín-Hurtado, Water Team leaders, Organisation for Economic Co-operation and Development (OECD)
- Peter Gleick, President and Jason Morrison, Water Program Leader, Pacific Institute
- Anders Berntell, Director General, and Jakob Granit, Program Director, Stockholm International Water Institute (SIWI)
- Jamal Saghir, Director, Energy, Water and Transport, Abel Mejia, Water Anchor Lead, and Michael Jacobsen, Senior Water Resources Specialist, World Bank Group
- Piet Klop, Acting Director, Markets and Enterprise Program, and Charles Iceland, Associate, People and Ecosystems Program, World Resources Institute (WRI)
- Dominic Waughray, Director of Environmental Initiatives, World Economic Forum (WEF), James Leape, CEO, Stuart Orr, Freshwater Manager, WWF-International, and Tom Le Quesne, Freshwater Policy Officer, WWF-UK

The team's first insight was to view water resources through an economic lens; that is, to analyze water supplies and their uses as they expend capital and recurring financial resources, and how water resources enable economic activity and growth. This "hydro-economic" analysis approach ultimately became the cornerstone of this early effort, as well as what ultimately became 2030 WRG.

The work began with a detailed analysis of water resources, in many cases to the sub-basin level, within major watersheds across the globe. This was coupled with population and economic development growth projections to determine existing water supplies and the projected gap to water resources in 2030. As previously illustrated in Figure 1.2, a 40 percent gap in water supplies, in the time and place needed, was projected.

The study then researched historical improvements in water productivity and increases in water supply. Both demand and supply were projected forward to 2030, with this historical data yielding a 60 percent gap in available supplies – "business as usual" improvement was deemed insufficient.

With clear facts supporting intuition that water supplies were under stress and could not meet all future growth demands, four locations were chosen: China, India, Republic of South Africa, and Sao Paulo state in Brazil.

Through comprehensive research and interviews, the team further refined water data, including costs on the supply and demand side, and growth plans across various sectors (such as industry, agriculture). An early insight was that to properly model water resources and economic growth, *energy and agriculture conditions and projections also needed to be fully evaluated.* This eventually led to the concept of the Nexus, which was also incubated in the Agenda Council.

After verifying data through socialization and review, water supply curves were developed for each location, as well as more detailed views at a more granular level as illustrated by the example of India provided in the WRG report.

In the words of Jamal Saghir (director, Energy, Transport and Water, World Bank), "This [approach] will get the water solutions discussion on the agenda of the CFOs and finance ministers," versus only the water, agriculture, and industry ministers, and their counterparts in the private sector.[3]

The results were published in *Charting Our Water Future: Economic Frameworks to Inform Decision-Making,* launched at the IFC's headquarters in Washington, DC, in November of 2009.[4]

The study's central thesis was that

while current water supply will be inadequate to meet the water requirements of the next two decades, meeting all competing demands for water is in fact possible at reasonable cost. However, achieving this outcome will require a concerted effort by all stakeholders, the willingness to adopt a total resource view where water is seen as a key, cross-sectoral input for development and growth, and the courage to undertake and fund long-needed reforms.[5]

A key innovation, beyond the hydro-economic perspective, was the active support and involvement of the private sector alongside traditional institutions and civil society.

Maturity

The report was further highlighted at various meeting and conferences including WEF's annual summit in Davos in the winter of 2010, generating keen interest from various governments and organizations seeking innovative approaches to water challenges.

The concept (as 2030 WRG was not yet an entity) was stewarded and advanced by WEF along with some of the members of the original study group and a growing list of supporters. Additional analyses (such as in Mexico and Jordan) were conducted to garner additional interest and support, as well as to refine and document the approach.

Culminating in mid-2012, 2030 WRG was formally instituted as an initiative within the IFC though with an independent Governing Council (GC) and Steering Board (SB). Founding members were:

- International Finance Corporation (IFC)
- World Bank Group
- Inter-American Development Bank (IDB)
- African Development Bank (AfDB)
- Global Water Partnership (GWP)
- Worldwide Fund for Nature (WWF)
- The Coca-Cola Company
- Nestlé S.A.
- SABMiller plc
- PepsiCo, Inc.
- World Economic Forum
- Global Green Growth Initiative (3GI)
- United Nations Development Program (UNDP)
- Swedish International Development Agency (Sida)
- Swiss Agency for Development and Cooperation (SDC)

The GC and SB were comprised of senior membership from these organizations.

A.C.T.

STEP 1	STEP 2	STEP 3
ANALYSIS to support better decisions	**C**ONVENING public-private-civil society stakeholders	**T**RANSFORMATION to higher performance and sustainability

 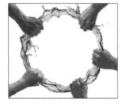 

Comprehensive fact base with broad agreement Cost, Benefit or Risk analysis depending on countries needs	**Multi-stakeholder platforms** to help government shape and take forward priority programs, plans and actions	**Concrete proposals** to ensure lasting change on the ground Can be Programs, Plans, but also concrete PPP proposals

Figure 4.1 **The ACT approach**

Source: 2030 WRG, *2016 Annual Report.*

2030 WRG then continued to expand efforts to include Peru, Mongolia, and the state of Karnataka, in India. Importantly, 2030 WRG codified the approach to country engagement with an Analyze (A), Convene (C), and Transform (T) approach – ACT (Figure 4.1):[6]

The ACT approach utilized and leveraged the following.

- The private sector, as they:
  - Are, collectively, the most important and largest water user both directly, as a manufacturing/producing industry, and indirectly, as producer or purchaser of agricultural products
  - Depend on the water resource for their operations and a society that develops and grows for their own development and growth, and realizes that water is a prerequisite for this growth
  - Have knowledge to share, nationally and internationally
  - Can act fast
  - Engage many politicians, who are willing to engage with them, and which can trigger action

- Hydro-economic analyses, since:

  o Decision-makers require decision support systems (DSSs) to manage the use of water resources in a more integrated, effective, and efficient way

  o Decision-makers want language and a platform for debating water policy choices, and DSS can simulate policy questions

  o Such analyses can transparently show costs and benefits of options – ensuring cost effectiveness and beneficial investments, empowering stakeholders and increasing transparency, presenting a clear view of water resources in the basin, stock, flow, how it's used, what's available for alternative uses, establishing a baseline and alternative values of water in use, and identifying opportunities for saving water and increasing its economic productivity

- Multi-stakeholder platforms, where:

  o Dialogue platforms are formed, where all involved actors would sit together, which is generally missing in most existing platforms

  o The private sector becomes willing to collaborate and share experience when they sit at the same table with each other (also with competitors), with government, and with civil society

  o Cost-effectiveness and pros and cons of different proposals are discussed

  o Government can make sure that proposals are developed in an open and transparent way, and that all concerned have been involved

Growth

The growth of 2030 WRG is important to reflect on, as it points to the success of the approach to be highlighted in the next section of this chapter. This growth can be measured at the global level in two ways: membership and locations.

New members in the private sector, joining Nestlé, PepsiCo, Coca-Cola (note: The Coca-Cola Company is a member and supporter of 2030 WRG. The author, Greg Koch, in his former role with The Coca-Cola Company, was a member of the Steering Board of 2030 WRG)

and ABInBev (ABInBev acquired SABMiller in 2016), are the Dow Chemical Company (Dow) and Grundfos, a leading supplier of water technologies. Among bilateral donors, the Hungarian government and Danish Green Growth have joined SDC and Sida. Joining the group of international non-governmental organizations (NGOs) and international government organizations (IGOs) are BRAC, a development organization dedicated to alleviating poverty by empowering the poor, and the International Union for Conservation of Nature (IUCN, which replaced WWF). The funding members of this collective group contribute over US$9.5 million to 2030 WRG annually.[7]

Locations have grown to the following:

- Mexico
- Peru
- Sao Paulo state, in Brazil
- Karnataka state, in India
- Maharashtra state, in India
- National and Uttar Pradesh engagement, in India, including the Ganges River
- Bangladesh
- Mongolia
- Vietnam
- Tanzania
- Kenya
- Ethiopia
- South Africa

Engagement in Jordan was suspended following the Arab Spring and civil unrest in the region (due to the Syrian conflict and refugees).

This growth has come with both maturity and recognition. In 2014, 2030 WRG commissioned the international consultancy Dalberg to conduct an evaluation of the effectiveness of the approach and recommend improvements, serving as input to 2030 WRG's strategic plan and budget. Through extensive research and interviews, both with 2030 WRG members and, importantly, numerous persons and organizations in the locations where 2030 WRG was active at the time, Dalberg was able to help strengthen 2030 WRG's value proposition and make key recommendations.

Citing Dalberg's report (an internal 2030 WRG document), key findings and recommendations were:

- The hydro-economic analysis is seen as an effective tool to engage senior decision-makers and trigger a public debate around water issues;
- 2030 WRG's convening efforts have successfully supported the development of multi-stakeholder work streams;

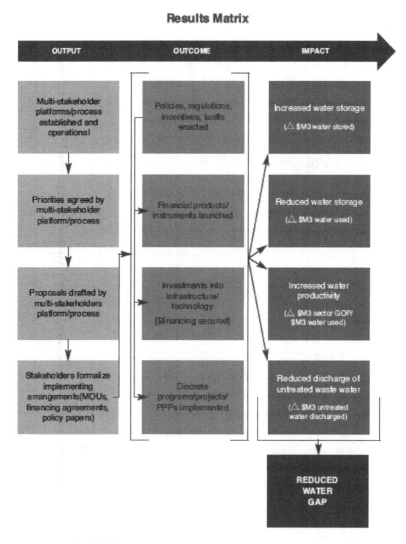

Figure 4.2 **2030 WRG results matrix**

Source: 2030 WRG, *2015 Annual Report.*

- They have defined clear indicators and targets;
- They have conducted a strategic mapping exercise and re-articulated 2030 WRG's theory of change and communicated it broadly;
- They have taken advantage of the development of the post-2015 agenda to give 2030 WRG a central role in the articulation of innovative public-private collaborations in the water sector;
- They have made organizational and process improvements.

The study was used to refine the strategic plan, influencing the way forward. Importantly, a results matrix was developed to track progress (see Figure 4.2).[8]

Growth can also be illustrated using the matrix in Table 4.1 and comparing progress.[9]

The formation and membership of MSPs in each location is a truer reflection of the uptake, growth, and success of 2030 WRG. The international corporations, NGOs, and IGOs listed above are important to support and steer efforts, as well as engage at the local level. However, much more important to long-term success is the engagement of such organizations and institutions locally, starting with the government. As an example, the MSPs for Peru number over 50, which is similar in depth and breadth for the other locations.

Much of the growth in members and locations can be attributed 2030 WRG's efforts at knowledge sharing and tool development, and direct engagement by various members as well as exposure and recognition at key forums such as WEF's regional summits and its annual conference in Davos, Switzerland.[10]

Table 4.1 **Growth and progress indicators**

Year	OPERATIONAL MULTI-STAKEHOLDER PLATFORMS (MSPS)	PRIORITY AREAS IDENTIFIED BY MSPS	PROJECT CONCEPTS DEVELOPED	FULL PROPOSALS	PROGRAMS UNDERWAY/ FINANCING SECURED
2015	9 with 297 local partners	33	28	15	5
2016	10 with 505 local partners	53	57	43	14

Source: 2030 WRG data.

As an example, in Davos in January 2017, a private session was convened by WEF entitled *Shaping a New Water Economy* which highlighted 2030 WRG and used its approach as a framework for discussion.[11] The session attracted some 50 leaders from governments, corporations, NGOs, and IGOs.

As of writing, 2030 WRG is in transition from the IFC to the Global Water Practice of the World Bank, to better leverage its staff and network of some 300 water professionals.

Progress

So what does progress look like? Below are examples across locations that demonstrate the effectiveness of 2030 WRG and local MSPs, each led by the government to evaluate tradeoffs and make progress to closing water supply gaps and helping ensure sustainable growth. The reader is encouraged to refer to 2030 WRG's annual reports and other documents which detail the ACT process and its developments along the way.[12]

Karnataka, India

A state-wide program for drip-irrigation in sugarcane has been formed in partnership with government, sugar companies, financial institutions, and technology vendors. The government has committed $250 million to the program (underway), which has the potential of resulting in 2.6 billion cubic meters less being water abstracted if 100 percent adopted by 700,000 farmers, representing 10 percent of the state's projected water demand-supply gap in 2030.

In addition, a new wastewater reuse/recycling policy framework has been developed, which would incentivize the reuse of treated municipal wastewater by industry. This is currently pending cabinet approval. According to S. Vishwanath, director of the Biome Environmental Trust, "Integrated, concerted efforts to conserve water are crucial. The equitable and sustainable wastewater reuse policy facilitated by the 2030 WRG and its multi-stakeholder partners will encourage political will, economic rationale, and social consensus in this direction."

Maharashtra, India

Five public-private-partnerships (PPPs) have been developed for integrated agriculture development across the state, instituting different cropping systems resulting in some 5.7 million cubic meters less water abstracted per year. This approach has a huge potential for scaling up in the state and across India.

Also, a program for climate-resilient cotton cultivation in drought-prone, rain-fed districts is under development in partnership with global brands, local buyers of cotton, the government, community organizations, and farmers to increase on-farm water security. The expected impact is on 500,000 farmers and $500 million financing facilitated, including potential Green Climate Fund allocation. If successful, this program will improve livelihoods for extremely vulnerable farmers. According to Alok Bhargava, the CEO of Nalanda Foundation "In drought-prone Aurangabad, we see a major role for the 2030 WRG's multi-stakeholder platform towards streamlining corporate social responsibility funds from the private sector and in accelerating project design and implementation."

South Africa

The "No Drop" program (funded and under implementation) will reduce municipal drinking water distribution system losses from 37 to 18 percent by 2025. It can save over 630 million cubic meters of water, equivalent to over 23 percent of the projected 2030 national water gap. The eight biggest metropolitan areas in South Africa are already committed, representing 90 percent of total municipal water supply in the republic.

A new program to increase water use efficiency in big irrigation schemes by improving allocation of water has already reduced water use by 48 million cubic meters in four irrigation schemes, representing 3 percent of the national water gap projected for 2030. This project also has a huge potential for scaling up in South Africa and globally in many locales. Nandha Govender of Eskom believes that

With increasing water stress compounded by the drought across Southern Africa, we need to conserve and use this limited and precious resource wisely to ensure water is accessible and affordable to all and of suitable quality. Eskom is actively reducing its freshwater footprint and managing its water use efficiently, but risks outside its control require a collective approach to ensure water security for electricity generation.

The SWPN provides a round-table platform for engagement, leading to collective solutions and action to manage shared water risks and common challenges.

Peru

A new system for prioritization of investments in water infrastructure has been formally adopted by the National Water Authority and the Ministry of Agriculture (made legally binding). Also, new regulations and tariffs for abstraction of groundwater by industry were developed and instituted. The tariffs are annual and not based on the volume of water used. However, the revenue will be used to fund regulator activities to collect and refine groundwater use data, establish sustainable use thresholds and options to increase supply or decrease demand. Fernando Momiy, president of the Board of Directors of SUNASS commented

> To comply with sustainable development goal 6 approved by the United Nations there is a need to move toward Integrated Management of Urban Water Resources. In Peru, responsibility for providing groundwater management & monitoring services has been transferred to Water Utilities in geographical areas where they operate and bill users of these water reserves a tariff for this service. SUNASS is responsible for developing a methodology for the calculation of a groundwater management & monitoring service tariff and setting for each operator. The 2030 WRG contributed in a decisive and fundamental manner to the design and development of the methodology and are performing a key role, both in supporting the water services regulator (SUNASS), as well as in the creation of the proper incentives for sustainable water use.

Elsa Galarza, minister of the Environment of Peru believes that

> Local and international experience has shown us that private sector engagement is a powerful tool for the acceleration of reforms and progress toward sustainable development. 2030 Water Resources Group plays a key role in Peru connecting

different sectors in society through open, transparent and results-oriented spaces for dialogue for the sustainable management of water.

Mongolia

The MSP developed a methodology for water valuation, leading to changes of tariffs for commercial water abstraction, smarter incentives for efficient water use and wastewater treatment. According to the engineer, B. Batsukh, of Ulaanbaatar Water Sewage and Supply Authority

> The hydro-economic analysis of Ulaanbaatar city conducted by the 2030 WRG has brought many new ideas for us. The 2030 WRG's help in prioritizing solutions enabled us to think outside the box, looking for innovative methods to address the challenges. I am looking forward to working with the 2030 WRG on the next steps.

While according to Ts Tumentsogt, CEO of Erdenes MGL

> The 2030 WRG's hydro-economic analysis of Gobi's coal regions has become an important tool, leading us in the right direction for water-related decision-making. We endorse and actively support the 2030 WRG's multi-pronged approach for mine water management to promote improved practices on the ground.

The Sustainable Development Goals

If we return to the central theme of abundance, we see in the Sustainable Development Goals (SDGs) a set of targets which, if delivered, would solve our most pressing challenges (e.g., poverty, hunger, poor health and education, pollution), deliver considerably on personal, social, and environmental well-being with abundance for many, and set the stage for sustainable existence and growth (where possible).

Even modest gains in any of the seventeen areas would result in significant benefits for mankind and ecosystems.

"If delivered" is the essential phrase: the SDGs are a starting point, a wish list, if you will, and, as Antoine de Saint-Exupéry put it *"A goal without a plan is just a wish."*[13]

One could then argue that a wholehearted, concerted effort by all governments to deliver on the SDGs is all that is needed. However, as we have shown, history and existing trends, the complexity of the Nexus, climate change, and an exponential growth in population and demands on resources require a careful plan to achieve the SDGs. This is not only to progress and achieve one given target but to do so in ways that do not make it more difficult (even impossible) to achieve another, and to do so cost-effectively.

This section will first look back at what was achieved for the Millennium Development Goals (MDGs). We will then outline the SDGs and some of the key challenges and interlinkages. We will end with our thoughts on the role of the private sector, including some examples, and a suggested framework for prioritization within policy decisions aimed to speed progress and help ensure success.

Millennium Development Goals

From earlier efforts, including the 2000 Millennium Summit at United Nations headquarters in New York,[14] the world's governments convened in 2005, with commitments from all 189 United Nations member states at that time, and at least 22 international organizations, to agree to the fulfilment of the following MDGs by 2015:[15]

1   To eradicate extreme poverty and hunger
2   To achieve universal primary education
3   To promote gender equality and empower women
4   To reduce child mortality
5   To improve maternal health
6   To combat HIV/AIDS, malaria, and other diseases
7   To ensure environmental sustainability
8   To develop a global partnership for development

Establishing and making progress against the MDGs led to global recognition of social and environmental challenges. This alone was an important step, as public awareness and debate are necessary for governments to effectively advance solutions. The MDGs were also important as a framework for business to shape its efforts in support of the goals.

As an example, the MDG goal on improving access to safe water and sanitation was a critical input into the inspiration and strategy for The Coca-Cola Company's 2009 goal to help establish safe water access for two million people in Africa by 2015,[16] through its Replenish Africa Initiative (RAIN). The company reported it exceeded its goal, reaching some 2.4 million people by the end of 2015. In 2013, Coca-Cola extended the goal to 2020, with a target of a cumulative six million people with access to safe drinking water.

There was mixed progress, globally, in achieving targets by the 2015 deadline but all progress should be heralded, as it generated resources, mobilized action, and, importantly, achieved considerable benefits to the lives and livelihoods of millions of people.

Below is a summary of overall global progress of the key components of each goal, with additional sub-goals as well as regional and country-level details found in UN reporting:[17]

MDG 1: Eradicate extreme poverty and hunger. Globally, the number of people living in extreme poverty declined by more than half, falling from 1.9 billion in 1990 to 836 million in 2015. The target of halving the proportion of people suffering from hunger was narrowly missed, from 23.3 percent in 1990–1992 to 12.9 percent in 2014–2016.

MDG 2: Achieve universal primary education. Primary school enrollment figures had a remarkable rise, but the goal of achieving universal primary education was just missed, with the net enrollment rate increasing from 83 percent in 2000 to 91 percent by the end of 2015.

MDG 3: Promote gender equality and empower women. Many more girls are now in school compared to 15 years ago. The developing regions as a whole have achieved the target of eliminating gender disparity in primary, secondary, and tertiary education. Women rose to make up 41 percent of paid workers outside the agricultural sector, an increase from 35 percent in 1990.

MDG 4: Reduce child mortality. The child mortality rate was reduced by more than half over the 25 years prior to 2015 – falling from 90 to 43 deaths per 1,000 live births – but it failed to meet the target of a drop of two-thirds.

MDG 5: Improve maternal health. Since 1990, the maternal mortality ratio declined by 45 percent worldwide (versus the two-thirds target), and most of the reduction has occurred since 2000.

MDG 6: Combat HIV/AIDS, malaria, and other diseases. The target of stopping and beginning to reverse the spread of HIV/AIDS by 2015 was not met, although the number of new HIV infections fell by around 40 percent between 2000 and 2013.

MDG 7: Ensure environmental sustainability. Some 2.6 billion people gained access to improved drinking water since 1990, so the target of reducing by 50 percent the number of people without access to improved sources of water was achieved. However, as of the end of 2015, 663 million people across the world still did not have access to improved drinking water. Worldwide, 2.1 billion people gained access to improved sanitation and the proportion of people practicing open defecation fell by almost half since 1990.

MDG 8: Develop a global partnership for development. Between 2000 and 2014, overseas development assistance from rich nations to developing countries increased by 66 percent in real terms, and in 2013 reached the record figure of $134.8 billion.

Despite the success on some of the goals, key disparities still exist:

- The poorest benefitted the least;
- Success in rural areas lags well behind urban areas;
- Climate change and conflict in many regions has reversed or stalled some of the progress.

Also, it is impossible to determine how much of the success that was achieved on the MDGs was due to new and concerted efforts to meet the goals versus business-as-usual improvement that one could expect over time. In addition, how much of the progress against some of the goals can be attributed to the growth of cellular telephone coverage and use, Internet penetration, access to information, and connection to solutions and supply chains?

In looking back on the progress made on the MDGs, we will not further explore what could have been; that is water under the proverbial bridge. As of 2017, the urgency of finding solutions for abundance and well-being are paramount. Lastly, the SDGs provide ample opportunity to achieve the MDGs and exceed their ambition.

This is a critical point and hints at the order of magnitude challenge the SDGs present over the MDGs. A comparison of the MDGs and SDGs also illustrates that in some areas, progress on a specific target without sufficient analysis of impacts on another area can create problems, worsen existing problems, or make an ultimate solution too costly to achieve.

For example, the SDG goal on water access addresses an important shortfall compared to the same MDG goal: the distinction is "access to *safe* water" versus "access to *improved* sources of water."

The MDG goal was defined, tracked, and progress reported by the Joint Monitoring Program (JMP).[18] The target for "improved" sources of water was defined as:

- Piped water into dwelling
- Piped water to yard/plot
- Public tap or standpipe
- Tube well or borehole
- Protected dug well
- Protected spring
- Rainwater

Again, having reached the goal, bringing access to such sources within reach of some 2.6 billion people is a cause for celebration. However, access to such an improved source of water does *not* ensure consumption that is protective of human health or the environment. Both are critical factors in water resource management.

If we use the World Health Organization's (WHO) guidelines for safe drinking water,[19] then it is estimated that some four billion people do not have access to such water.[20] This far exceeds a cursory reflection of the MDG on water access, which could suggest that we have less than 700 million people yet to serve.

It is the author's experience that many organizations and speakers inadvertently or incompletely report progress on water access as "safe" versus "improved." For example, water.org's website reports "663 million people – 1 in 10 – lack access to safe water."[21] WaterAid also reports the same statistic in its annual report.[22]

A good example of the dangers of declaring victory in achieving access to improved sources of water is Bangladesh. Efforts beginning in the 1970s to install numerous groundwater wells to provide drinking water were called "the largest poisoning of a population in history."[23] Many of the millions of tube wells installed in mainly shallow groundwater tapped water naturally containing high concentrations of arsenic. As a result, millions of people have experienced and are at risk of skin lesions, various cancers, and other long-term health impacts.

SDG Goal 6.1 addresses this shortfall, with the goal being "achieve universal and equitable access to safe and affordable drinking water for all."[24] In the meantime, how many people are drinking water delivered through MDG action that could be affecting their health? And how many "improved" sources of water need to be revisited and potentially modified to deliver "safe" drinking water?

SDG Goal 6.4 hints at an additional potential problem with the progress made on the MDGs. The goal states "ensure sustainable withdrawals and supply of freshwater to address water scarcity and substantially reduce the number of people suffering from water scarcity." Improved water sources tapped to deliver on the MDG goal may now be stressed beyond their sustainable supply due to increased water use; many may have been so stressed *before* being tapped and now unsustainable use is accelerated.

SDG Goal 6.3 points to yet another challenge: "improve water quality by reducing pollution, eliminating dumping and minimizing release of hazardous chemicals and materials, halving the proportion of untreated wastewater and substantially increasing recycling and safe reuse globally." Improved water sources provided during the MDG era, even if assumed "safe" and sustainable, may have become contaminated from discharge of untreated sewage to the raw water source area. Given that the MDG goal of improved sanitation was not met and that 80 percent of industrial and domestic sewage in the developing world is discharged with little to no treatment,[25] the likelihood for such impact is considerable.

This analysis of MDG and SDG goals on water, while incomplete, points to similar challenges that potentially exist in progress made for other MDG goals. For instance, is world support in the developing world at risk due to budget constraints? Have efforts to deliver additional food been made sustainable and affordable over the long term with regard to the sources of crops and the supply chains to deliver them? This is a sobering reflection on the MDGs and a wake-up call for what is in store to meet the SDGs.

Sustainable Development Goals

In September of 2015, the United Nations announced the result of years of research and debate by numerous working groups and evaluation of input from all sectors of society by launching the SDGs. These 17 goals apply to everyone and seek to mobilize efforts globally, through 2030, to solve significant problems, from poverty and climate change to water and inequalities of many forms.

The SDGs, officially known as "*Transforming Our World: The 2030 Agenda for Sustainable Development*" has 169 targets within the 17 goals:

1 End poverty in all its forms everywhere
2 End hunger, achieve food security and improved nutrition, and promote sustainable agriculture
3 Ensure healthy lives and promote well-being for all at all ages
4 Ensure inclusive and equitable quality education and promote lifelong learning opportunities for all
5 Achieve gender equality and empower all women and girls
6 Ensure availability and sustainable management of water and sanitation for all

7 Ensure access to affordable, reliable, sustainable, and modern energy for all
8 Promote sustained, inclusive, and sustainable economic growth, full and productive employment, and decent work for all
9 Build resilient infrastructure, promote inclusive and sustainable industrialization and foster innovation
10 Reduce inequality within and among countries
11 Make cities and human settlements inclusive, safe, resilient, and sustainable
12 Ensure sustainable consumption and production patterns
13 Take urgent action to combat climate change and its impacts
14 Conserve and sustainably use the oceans, seas, and marine resources for sustainable development
15 Protect, restore, and promote sustainable use of terrestrial ecosystems, sustainably manage forests, combat desertification, and halt and reverse land degradation, and halt biodiversity loss
16 Promote peaceful and inclusive societies for sustainable development, provide access to justice for all and build effective, accountable, and inclusive institutions at all levels
17 Strengthen the means of implementation and revitalize the global partnership for sustainable development

Meeting all the goals for SDG 6 does seem daunting. However, we feel that despite the challenges and significant threats, we should remain optimistic, yet grounded in the reality of what we can achieve.

To *achieve* the goals:

- Businesses must drive sustainable solutions at scale, while linking development goals to core business interests, identifying and managing their impact and collaborating with governments and civil society.
- Governments must show strong leadership in overcoming silos, ensuring adequate funding and accountability towards political commitments, strengthening institutions, acting as regulators and setting incentives to ensure cost-effective solutions and good management.

- Academia also needs to overcome silos and look to educate students with a broad, multidisciplinary understanding of challenges and interlinkages across many topics.
- Civil society needs to consider more partnerships with each other and with government and business. They may also need to focus on fewer things with the goal of greater impact.
- Citizens need to prepare for change by seeking to better understand the challenges facing us all. They need to actively engage their governments and seek to advocate for the future they want.

In the following section we will dive deeper on the role of business and government, but here we will outline some of the key interlinkages and challenges in meeting the SDGs.

Many have commented on two SDG goals as being paramount. The first is climate change (Goal 13) which many see as the fundamental challenge facing the Earth. Our premise is that the Nexus supersedes climate change, with global warming being a force multiplier but we will use climate change to signal the scale and complexity of the work ahead.

Goal 17, partnerships, is seen by many the key to solving the challenges.

Here we agree wholeheartedly: the scale and interconnectedness of the problems we face, the goals and the 2030 deadline we have set for ourselves require partnerships across knowledge, project design and execution, technology, supplies, financing, and education.

Beyond this "paramount" challenge and approach to solutions, key interlinkages exist between the SDGs, including:

- Ending hunger and universal access to safe drinking water are fundamental to achieving other goals, such as ending poverty, and sustaining progress on other goals such as education: the best school and teachers can't educate a young girl who is hungry or out sick due to water-borne disease from unsafe water.
- Ending poverty is needed to provide a healthy, educated workforce to sustain infrastructure and environmental

conservations in both manpower and the tax revenue from gainful employment.

- Gender equality first in education then employment is needed to make full use of everyone's talents and abilities.

Beyond the challenges, scope, cost, and magnitude of ambition that the SDGs present, along with the reality of the Nexus, resource demands, and the need to make tough decisions, there are some additional factors that require attention, as they have and will present difficulties in meeting the SDGs:

- The SDGs themselves and the 2030 deadline are self-created and self-imposed, with little to no real consequences for those accountable to delivering them if they are not met. That is, a politician may not get re-elected if she fails to reduce poverty, but the voting public would likely think of poverty in personal terms versus UN goals. As such, efforts could be directed to what a politician thinks will help most for his or her own cause. A good example is weight loss: how many of us have set a goal to reduce weight and failed? Yes, your longer term health remains at risk as a result but there is no accountability to others or consequences as such.
- There is a much clearer understanding that the SDGs apply to every country while the MDGs were thought to apply only to the developing world. This can have major ramifications on the ability of one country to assist others. Take, for example, the United States, which does not have universal access to safe drinking water or sanitation. Its ability to help other countries progress on SDG Goal 6.1 is diminished to some extent by the efforts it will need to expend to achieve its own goal.
- There remain both "unspeakable" and "unhearable" topics that will challenge progress. Gender equity is taboo, even prohibited in many forms, in several countries (Goal 5). Lesbian, gay, bisexual, and transgender rights are not universal, and are even outlawed in many places (Goal 8). There exists widespread hesitation and reluctance to speak of fecal sludge management and menstrual hygiene (Goal 6) in many cultures. Climate change acceptance remains a debated topic politically in a few locales (Goal 13).

Key to combatting these difficulties will be an improved understanding and respect for different cultures, their form of government, and the depth and repute of their academic institutions – something the authors feel was missing in many MDG efforts.

Another key will be to have a greater appreciation and dedication of resources for training, long-term operation, and monitoring solutions (such as a safe water access system) versus the mostly initial capital costs and technology used. Put another way, the "soft stuff" *is* the "hard stuff."

We must also look beyond traditional boundaries to solving problems. For example, the watershed, "policy-shed," and "problem-shed" are all different when you look at the Jordan River Valley, in the Levant. Professor Shafiqul Islam, with Tufts University, advocates for creating a new space for solutions that may be useful in tackling such challenges where a previously unknown space for solutions is created to the mutual benefit of all involved. The story is of three brothers given an inheritance of 17 camels from their father with what seems to be an impossible mandate of their division among the three.[26] The "creation" of an 18th camel provides the solution and points us to the need for new ways of thinking that we will explore in the closing Chapter 5.

The role of the private sector

Throughout this book, we have argued strongly for partnerships, including business partnering with governments, each other (peers and even competitors), as well as civil society in addressing challenges, SDG goal progress or otherwise. However, governments and other stakeholders need to be careful in their assumptions about what the private sector can deliver and what it can afford.

First comes the playing field. That is, efforts by the private sector cannot proceed without the stage being set by government to harness, direct, and amplify what the private sector seeks to accomplish.

A good example can be found in Cabo Verde where the Millennium Challenge Corporation (MCC),[27] an independent US foreign aid agency, is funding a $41 million safe water access, sanitation, and hygiene (WASH) effort with the local government.[28] The compact is that the government does not provide funds to connect households to the water infrastructure being constructed. As part of Coca-Cola's Replenish Africa Initiative (RAIN),[29] The Coca-Cola Africa Foundation provided some $200,000, investing alongside MCC in order to help up to 20,000 low-income households gain access to the water network. The "stage was set" by the government and MCC to allow for maximum impact from Coca-Cola's investment. Had Coca-Cola invested the same funds in separate efforts on WASH, though welcome by those that such an investment could reach, they most certainly would not have reached 20,000 households.

Second is the scale of investment required. *Fortune Magazine* estimates the net profits of the top 500 private businesses to be $840 billion in 2016. The World Bank estimates that extending basic WASH services to the unserved will cost $28.4 billion (range: $13.8 to $46.7 billion) per year from 2015 to 2030.[30] This is a cumulative total of nearly $880 billion over that 16-year timeframe. Asking the private sector to provide funding for just SDG Goal 6.1 would require 500 corporations, all subject to boards of directors, and most to shareowners, to contribute some one-third of profits for 16 years.

For a similar perspective on the scale of government versus private sector budgets, as well as the magnitude of investment required to sustainably achieve certain goals, turn to the March 2011 TED Talk by Bill Gates.[31]

All that said, the private sector does have an important role to play. One could argue that role will fundamentally change the nature of many corporations to be more aligned with societal needs and government growth plans.

The role of the private sector starts in their direct operations – getting and keeping your house in order. It then should mature up and down the value chain seeking to influence, even require, suppliers to adhere to more sustainable practices, from water management to gender equality, and address the full lifecycle of their products in the marketplace and beyond.

It also requires businesses to step out of their direct operations and value chain to address shared challenges in the communities and ecosystems they cohabitate with others.

An example from Coca-Cola shows its thoughts on efforts aligned across SDG 6 (water), from direct operations and across its value chain.[32]

Table 4.2 **SDGs and Coca-Cola's alignment and targets**

SDG target	Coca-Cola alignment/support
By 2030, achieve universal and equitable access to safe and affordable drinking water for all	A key part of our water stewardship strategy with sustainable communities is RAIN, bringing safe water to six million people by 2020
By 2030, achieve access to adequate and equitable sanitation and hygiene for all, and end open defecation, paying special attention to the needs of women and girls and those in vulnerable situations	Many of our safe water projects also address sanitation and hygiene, with a focus on females, especially in adolescent-aged school settings
By 2030, improve water quality by reducing pollution, eliminating dumping, and minimizing release of hazardous chemicals and materials, halving the proportion of untreated wastewater and substantially increasing recycling and safe reuse globally	We require full treatment of process wastewater before discharge to the local environment, even when not mandated by local regulation, and have achieved 99.9 percent compliance with this strict standard. Also, our water efficiency program seeks to maximize water reuse in our plants and local communities
By 2030, substantially increase water-use efficiency across all sectors and ensure sustainable withdrawals and supply of freshwater to address water scarcity and substantially reduce the number of people suffering from water scarcity	We have improved water efficiency in our operations each year for 14 years towards a 25 percent improvement goal by 2020. We share best practices in water efficiency and reuse with other business through platforms such as the Beverage Industry Environmental Roundtable
	Our Source Water Protection Program is designed to ensure that our plants do not negatively impact the ability of others to access a sufficient quantity and quality of water. It goes further to require that plants engage others to seek solutions in situations where water allocation and use is unsustainable
	Lastly, our Sustainable Agriculture Guiding Principles (SAGPs) require total water use be reduced by implementing water saving practices, including water reuse and recycling where possible, and, where irrigation is used, implement the most efficient system as is technically available and financially affordable

(continued)

Table 4.2 *(continued)*

SDG target	Coca-Cola alignment/support
By 2030, implement integrated water resources management (IWRM) at all levels, including through transboundary cooperation, as appropriate	Our Source Water Protection program uses IWRM as a framework for holistic solutions by all water users across a shared watershed. IWRM is also a key component of the solution set proposed for water policy reform in our efforts with the 2030 Water Resources Group
By 2020, protect and restore water-related ecosystems, including mountains, forests, wetlands, rivers, aquifers, and lakes	In addition to helping communities and ecosystems adapt to a changing climate, ecosystem conservation is the primary way we achieve progress on our Replenish goal. The current estimate is that our watershed protection projects implemented by the end of 2016 are providing a Replenish benefit of approximately 221 billion liters per year. In addition, these projects are estimated to reduce sediment yield in 2016 by over 2.6 million metric tons per year and approximately 87.7 metric tons of other pollutants, such as pesticides and nutrients
By 2030, expand international cooperation and capacity-building support to developing countries in water- and sanitation-related activities and programs, including water harvesting, desalination, water efficiency, wastewater treatment, recycling, and reuse technologies	We openly share the details of all of our water projects, not only in the spirit of transparency but, hopefully, to inspire others to act and to share best practices, as well as lessons learned. Our partnerships, especially with WWF and UNDP, are designed to share, scale, and replicate solutions. With the most global of footprints, operating in all but two countries (Cuba and North Korea), we are able to leverage our experience and take action on water globally
Support and strengthen the participation of local communities in improving water and sanitation management	Community engagement is a hallmark of our approach to water projects. Our non-export, local production and sales business model makes our plants a part of the local community and helps strengthen the community's ownership of water access and conservation efforts we support

Source: The Coca-Cola Company, 2017.

Several other companies have made similar analyses and commitments to align future efforts with SDG execution, including Unilever,[33] Nestlé, and Tesco.[34]

In addition, there are several multi-stakeholder platforms among business that advocate and help enable collective action on sustainable development, including the CEO Water Mandate's *Guide to Water-related Collective Action*[35] and its *Guide to Responsible Business Engagement with Water Policy*.[36] The World Business Council on Sustainable Development (WBCSD) has the WASH at the Workplace Pledge,[37] while the Consumer Goods Forum has a collective and individual member goal of no net deforestation.[38]

Much more can be done and is even called for in the SDGs: the private sector can become a financier, shifting trillions of dollars of capital toward developing economies. And it can play an important role as an implementer, translating profits into sustained economic growth, social inclusion, and environmental protection. The principles underpinning such measures are anchored in SDG target 12.6, which encourages companies, especially large and transnational companies, to adopt sustainable practices and to integrate sustainability information into their reporting cycle.[39]

To that end, the UN recently announced the formation of a partnership platform to generate financing solutions for the SDGs.[40] This is welcome, as the finance, insurance, and re-insurance sector has the ability not only to provide loans but provide positive incentives to business strategically focused on sustainable development.

Prioritization framework for policy

Limited success on the MDGs, Nexus and resource demand challenges in a changing climate, a daunting list of SDGs, tough decisions to make, and a countdown underway to 2030 – with only 13 years left. What is a policymaker to do?

We have already reviewed, in Chapter 1, the shortcomings of past approaches and business as usual. Chapter 2 focused on the relatively new challenges of the Nexus and climate change. Making difficult decisions and weighing tradeoffs were the subjects of Chapter 3. Deep breath indeed, but we urge the reader to consider the focus of this book: well-being and abundance – and this chapter: opportunities.

As overwhelming as they seem (and as we have likely presented them), the SDGs are, in fact, an opportunity. Often the hardest part of a complex problem is determining what the problem actually is. You can debate to no end how we got where we are but the SDGs provide a clear outline of what needs to happen from here.

As the quote at the start if this chapter shows, now you need a plan of action. You know what needs to happen; now figure out how.

The first step is education of self. This book has outlined the global picture with some examples of specific countries and topics. The policymaker should first seek to determine where he or she is, relative to the targets of the SDGs. Those in the developing world will find a partial scorecard in their ultimate report on MDG progress. Those in the developed world may have similar data but all will need an honest accounting of where they stand today. This must also be done projected forward to account for resource demand and population growth, as well as accounting for uncertainty due to climate change.

The next step is to educate others. That is, are your superiors, peers, constituency, and other stakeholders similarly aware of the challenges, growth plans, goals, and specific targets? If not, you need to play an active role in helping educate them.

Next is to enlist help. No one policymaker, agency, or ministry, especially in a Nexus world, can hope to find solutions in a vacuum. One must reach not only across the aisle, but across the street, around the block and downstairs. Such outreach need not, should not, lead only to others in government. Reach out to business, civil society, academia, and the general public – ask for help and form partnerships. In most places, widespread smartphone and Internet coverage allows unprecedented ability to inform, solicit opinions, and seek collaboration.

As with any complex problem, solutions start and proceed one step at a time. Earlier in this chapter we outlined a recommendation for prioritization. Hunger, malnutrition, the lack of safe drinking water, and inadequate education resonate with any voter, and are already part of most plans. Progressing on solving these will build a background of policy "wins," instill confidence and build momentum, and lay the foundation for more healthy people actively contributing to society.

The literature and the world of debate on the SDGs are rife with frameworks and lists of priorities, from water access to gender equality and climate change mitigation to ecosystem restoration. No doubt these differ among countries and even sub-populations therein.

However, a careful analysis reveals that most of the proposed policy approaches share hallmarks that aim to deliver on SDG Goal 17.6 – enhance policy coherence for sustainable development. This sub-goal addresses the processes and means to solutions, not the ultimate outcome of various goals. This is critical for the policymaker and SDG success overall.

The OECD presents the concept of Policy Coherence for Sustainable Development (PCSD).[41] "It aims to increase governments' capacities to achieve the following objectives:"

1   Foster synergies across economic, social, and environmental policy areas
2   Identify tradeoffs and reconcile domestic policy objectives with internationally agreed objectives
3   Address the spillovers of domestic policies

It can help facilitate the design and implementation of policies to consider the:

1   Diversity, roles, and responsibilities of different actors as well as sources of finance – public and private, domestic and international
2   Policy inter-linkages across economic, social, and environmental areas, including the identification of synergies and tradeoffs
3   Non-policy drivers, i.e. the enablers and disablers at global, national, local, and regional levels for sustainable development outcomes
4   Policy effects, i.e. transboundary and temporal impacts.

In this context, the OECD presents a new definition for SDG Goal 17.6 that is a powerful construct for policymakers:[42]

Strengthen the capacity of governments to implement coherent and mutually-supportive policies, to achieve the SDGs in time to inform national action plans for SDG implementation, in ways that balance economic, social and environmental goals; consider domestic and international effects of policies; and support long-term sustainability.

Climate change adaption – resiliency

Unfortunately, we are facing the impacts of climate change now, and while mitigation must be pursued, we need aggressive investment in adaptation and resiliency. As former UN General Secretary Ban Ki-moon stated, "We must turn the greatest collective challenge facing humankind today, climate change, into the greatest opportunity for common progress towards a sustainable future."[43]

There is much research, modeling, and uncertainty as to what the future holds. Nations are working to mitigate the forecasted impacts, through the slowing, reduction, and even reversal of greenhouse gas emissions. Some impacts forecasted by a changed climate, such as rising sea levels and the frequency and intensity of storms, are already being experienced.

A warming planet does indeed equate to higher average temperatures. But the most obvious, widespread and impactful consequences will manifest in water. Rising sea levels, storm intensity, but also a shift in patterns of rainfall, with some dry areas becoming wetter and wet regions becoming more arid. Along with the intensity of storms, the duration of droughts is also predicted to lengthen.

The one, and perhaps only, bright spot in this otherwise gloomy outlook is that much of what we need to do to prepare and adapt to the changing and more unpredictable water situations are the same things we need to do anyway in addressing existing water challenges. Proactive water stewardship can go a long way to help many communities become less vulnerable and more resilient to climate change. These concepts, vulnerability and resilience, are important to distinguish in the context of climate change. And, again, there is need today to address these, with climate change amplifying the extent and immediacy of action.

Vulnerability is, in large part, a measure or assessment of how sensitive a community is to impacts from climate change, both in the context of its setting and exposure. Resilience focuses on that community's ability to cope with, adapt and recover, and, at a higher order, transform, from the impacts it faces. Put together, reducing vulnerability and increasing resilience are often considered as a community's "adaptive capacity."

Similar concepts apply to ecosystems, their vulnerability and resilience.

It is important understand these terms as solutions to improve. Each can look different – reforesting an area to reduce vulnerability to impacts of flood with adequate emergency services in place to help rebound from a flood, increasing resilience. Solutions can also look the same – more inclusive governance with strong capacity of regulators can help reduce vulnerability by carefully managing land use, such as logging, and at the same increase resilience when responding to extreme events.

Each can also involve "hard" solutions (reforestation, water infrastructure) and "soft" solutions (capacity-building, communication channels, awareness-raising). These solutions are dependent on the specific community or system and its vulnerability or resilience to climate change.

An energy policy focused on renewable technologies, a land use policy, and a water stewardship program can decrease a community's vulnerability to emerging climatic conditions.[44]

Adaptive capacity in energy and agriculture

Land that has been intensely logged and is now barren of trees and forest growth does a poor job of holding topsoil, slowing water flows, and allowing for the natural recharge of groundwater. The result? Fast-moving water, a lot of it, carrying precious soil and nutrients, flooding downstream communities and ecosystems. There are many good reasons today to justify planting trees, and there are many places that are reforesting land, afforesting (creating forests where there were none), removing non-native vegetation, reconnecting flood plains, and more. These are the very same actions needed for adaptation, but needed in greater quantities, faster.

A paper from the California Climate Change Center analyzes various models used to explore water management adaptation strategies for the year 2050.[45] Two models, California Value Integrated Network (CALVIN) and Energy-Based Hydropower Optimization Model (EBHOM), were used to optimize California's water supply system and high-elevation hydropower systems. In order to compare the effects of temperature and precipitation, both models considered the warming and drying effects of climate change as well as just the warming scenario. In this particular study, the warm-dry scenario represented a temperature increase of 4.5°C and an 18 percent reduction in precipitation throughout the state of California.[46] The warm-only scenario was based on historical mean annual runoff.

CALVIN assesses the effects of statewide temperature rise on water allocation and low-elevation hydropower generation. The model includes water treatment infrastructure, surface and groundwater reservoirs, and California's agricultural and urban demand areas.[47] After modeling the predicted water demand for 2050, the study found that the cost of water scarcity for agricultural purposes is higher in the presence of climate change. The urban water use penalty was lower than that of agricultural uses, due to a higher willingness to pay, but, when compared to the historical climate, statewide water shortages increased by 2.7 percent in a warm-only scenario and by 473 percent in a warm-dry scenario.[48] Additionally, when compared to the historical climate, the model yielded a 4.52 percent increase in operating costs and 4.50 percent decrease in hydropower benefits for the warm-dry scenario.[49]

EBHOM models the impact that climate change has on high-elevation hydropower systems throughout California. It consists of more than 150 hydropower plants, which are low-storage, high-head reservoirs and are not considered in CALVIN.[50] In the warm-dry scenario, energy generation decreased by 19.3 percent, and the average revenue from hydroelectricity generation decreased by 12 percent and 1 percent for the warm-dry and warm-only climate scenarios, respectively.[51]

Through this study, it is clear that precipitation has a larger impact on water scarcity and the economic repercussions of climate change. Agricultural processes are more susceptible to water shortages and revenue losses will occur for both low- and high-elevation hydropower plants.[52] However, not all regions will experience climate change the same way.

Two factors that determine the need and success of climate adaptation are a system's vulnerability and resilience. Vulnerability is a product of scale, variability, and residence time.[53] Scale represents a system's ability to buffer responses. For example, a large river will take a longer time to experience drought when compared to a smaller stream. Small systems will respond more rapidly to climate change, and so are considered more vulnerable.

Variability constitutes the idea of a system being permanent or temporary. For example, species that are dependent on *temporary* freshwater resources are more likely to more readily adapt to a changing climate, as opposed to those relying on a *permanent* water source.[54] Finally, a higher residence time relates to lower vulnerability. If a community relies on snowmelt and groundwater, it will have more stability and less vulnerability, making it more adaptable, despite a shift in the timing of melting or monsoon seasons.

The *Policy Brief* by the Cluster Group in Climate, Water, and Vulnerability hosted by the Swedish Water House discusses a case study involving farmers in the Thukela river basin in South Africa.[55] The farmers experienced obstacles such as lack of access to financing for equipment, which increased their vulnerability to climate change. Both small-scale and commercial farmers experienced challenges in water management adaptation, but the nature of the challenges stemmed from differing pre-conditions. Small-scale farmers did not have enough knowledge about agricultural technologies, while commercial farmers lacked trust in government officials in order to attain required permits.[56] In this case study, it is apparent that people can be vulnerable to climate change because of limited access to basic social services, exclusion from the decision-making process, or living in poorer, environmentally barren regions, where availability of natural resources is restricted. Therefore, programs and policies concerning climate adaptation must acknowledge the variability of needs and conditions for each stakeholder.

In order to incorporate effective climate adaptation processes in agriculture and energy generation, crop prices and storage capacities of energy plants may need to change. The cost of water scarcity or shortage for agriculture may be buffered by an increase in crop prices or by planting crops that are less water-extensive. Additionally, global warming will yield changes in monthly hydro-electricity generation.[57] However, storage capacity and generation rates can compensate for low-value months. By increasing a plant's energy storage and efficiency, enough energy can be generated to account for decreased water supply, thus decreasing the system's vulnerability.

Adaptive capacity in coastal zone management

Hurricanes and typhoons that we have faced for ages bring intense rainfall and tidal surges that often severely damage coastal communities. Research and practice has shown that well-preserved, natural coastal defenses, such as mangroves, vegetated sand dunes, and smart development, respectful of the environment, can go a long way in helping reduce the impacts of such storms, and allowing the ecosystem to recover more quickly. Many places are in need of such restoration of their natural defenses and adopting more resilient development practices. It works, it's needed today, and it's just the type of action needed to adapt to rising sea levels and more-intense rainfall events from a changing climate.

Not everything that needs to be done and is being done today exhausts the need for adaptation. Among the many considerations we all need to plan for are: early warning systems, more detailed and shared data collection and analyses, increased storage of water (to mitigate flood impacts and save water for dry periods), enhanced emergency response preparedness, water policy and governance that is flexible, allowing rapid modification to deal with rapid change (along with strong institutional capacity to manage such change), and preservation of areas of high cultural and biodiversity value (that may become flooded).

As stated before, climate change impacts are here and now. In the US, over $100 billion in infrastructure and 500,000 people are currently at risk from increased coastal flooding.[58] A projected $15 billion, plus annual maintenance fees, will be needed for adaptation costs to protect current infrastructure.[59]

To increase the resiliency of coastal regions, communities can construct flood protection infrastructure, increase riparian areas and upstream storage, restore and maintain wetlands, and improve the forecasting methods used for flooding.[60] Resilience is also increased through the study of how floods travel through catchments, and by focusing on risk-reduction strategies like accommodation.[61]

Adaptive capacity in water infrastructure

Communities currently lacking adequate infrastructure to capture, store, treat, and distribute clean drinking water are facing significant challenges today. If water flows become more unpredictable, whether higher (floods) or lower (droughts), then these challenges will become that much harder. There is a clear case for universal access to water and sanitation today, globally. Climate change is a strong motivator to act faster as well as smarter to reach this goal, with design for flexibility and redundancy in such infrastructure needed to handle the uncertainties.

The *Policy Brief* by the Cluster Group in Climate, Water, and Vulnerability hosted by the Swedish Water House also provides several methods for increasing a community's resilience. The common element focuses on improving access to water and ecosystem services, and the options include expanding rainwater harvesting, adopting water transfer schemes, restoring aquatic habitats, increasing water storage capacity, and improving water efficiency.[62]

As stated before, vulnerability and resiliency are the measurements of adaptive capacity. Specifically, climate adaptation is defined as the process of avoiding risk and facilitating change associated with emerging climate regimes. Adaptive or "vulnerability" thinking should be differentiated from "impacts" thinking.[63]

Vulnerability thinking promotes flexibility, is a continuous process, requires long-term planning, and should assess the resilience of ecological and institutional systems.[64]

WWF proposes eight elements for an adaptive water strategy:

1   Develop institutional capacity,
2   Create flexible allocation systems and agreements
3   Reduce external non-climate pressures
4   Help species and communities move their ranges
5   Think carefully about water infrastructure
6   Institute sustainable flood management policies
7   Support climate-aware government and development planning
8   Improve monitoring and responsiveness capacity

The first element, developing an institutional capacity, refers to controlling and monitoring legal and illegal water use, assessing physical and biophysical states and changes of freshwater systems, pollution prevention, and regulation of water infrastructure development and maintenance.[65]

Due to lower precipitation's diminished contribution to freshwater systems due to climate change, the availability of water will decrease. Water rights policies will need to be flexible and communicated for the sake of the social response to climate change. Traditional allocation methods may not be sufficient for the future, and must also incorporate economic activities.[66]

Nutrient pollution is an example of an external non-climate pressure that should be eliminated for the development of an adaptive water strategy. Freshwater ecosystems are limited by nutrients like phosphorous and nitrogen, which also impact our water quality.[67]

The fourth element WWF proposes encourages the response of species and economic systems by increasing their range. For example, species may be forced to relocate due to the effects of climate change (which calls for maintaining and increasing biological corridors to facilitate safe migration).

The development and management of water infrastructure should be responsive to a changing climate. The assumption that a hydrological system is stationary and takes on historical characteristics may not yield results appropriate for the future.[68] As discussed previously, there is uncertainty about future hydrology, which impacts infrastructure design and performance. Current systems should be modified and new systems should be designed with consideration of emerging hydrological patterns. If adaptive thinking is utilized in the management of these technologies, our options for the future may not be as limited.

The next element refers to increasing resilience when faced with predicted climatic events resulting from global warming. Flooding is expected to increase in many parts of the world, so the utilization of floodplains and washlands and strategically locating new developments contribute to adaptive water strategies.[69]

The last elements of an effective adaptive water strategy link government awareness to climate change and vulnerability assessments. Hydrological, ecological, and social variables must be monitored for high-stress situations so that communities can effectively respond without the introduction of conflict.[70] Government, economic, and social plans must be aware of climate change and the uncertainty that results in the freshwater system.

The crucial component for each of these elements is flexibility; due to the uncertainty in climate modeling, one must have the ability to adapt to variable climatic conditions. This flexibility incorporates increased resiliency and decreased vulnerability, to produce a more effective climate adaptation strategy. The extent that declined precipitation in arid regions or increased flood risk in temperate regions can only be predicted through models, adaptive thinking is necessary when implementing an effective water strategy for the future.

Failing to incorporate climate adaptation into water infrastructure

Perhaps the classic and most far-reaching example of failure to incorporate climate change into water management is, *in hindsight of course*, the Colorado River Compact. The Compact was originally negotiated in 1922 and allocated water resources based on limited data on flow and precipitation patterns.[71] In December 2007, climate models of changing water patterns and availability were not included in the interim agreement for the Compact. Now, climate models yield future drought along the Colorado River, making the new Compact irrelevant.[72] This issue introduces the possibility of stakeholder lawsuits, interstate conflicts, and a need for a new climate-aware compact.[73]

This example also shows one of the three freshwater impacts that climate change will bring: quantity depletion. Changes in precipitation patterns will influence water quality, quantity, and timing.[74] Water quality is defined as how appropriate an ecosystem's water is for use, and water *quantity* relates to the water volume of this ecosystem. Water timing is the expected change in water quantity over a time period.[75]

The California wine industry is another example of the need for climate adaptation. California's freshwater supply is dependent on snowmelt from the mountains of the Sierra Nevada.[76] As the snowpack decreases and the economic demand increases, there is pressure to change plant species in yards and gardens, and the California wine industry is predicted to move north, into Oregon and Washington.[77] Without modifying infrastructure, land, and water use policies, the adaptive capacity of these systems is inadequate, which will influence societal and economic productivity.

Climate adaptation in developing communities

These impacts are not specific to developed communities. Although developed communities will focus on climate adaptation through modifying infrastructure to decrease vulnerability, developing communities will adapt to climate change through autonomous adaptation.[78] In these circumstances, conditions other than climate change are more important, and adaptation methods may include increasing the community's resilience by improving access to water and ecosystem services. The focus should be on reducing poverty, encouraging diverse lifestyles, and protecting property resources.[79] Here, increased resilience to climate change is an additional effect of improving water and sanitation systems, because water is the main factor for the well-being and resilience of communities.[80]

For this specific approach, four principles for IWRM were established.[81] IWRM was presented at the International Conference on Water and Environment in Dublin, and includes capturing societal perspectives, modifying planning strategies, conducting land and water resources management, and providing for the protection and remediation of natural systems. The four principles are:

1   Freshwater is a finite and vulnerable resource, and is vital for life and the environment.
2   Water development and management should involve the participation of users, planners, and policymakers.
3   Women play a central part in the provision, management, and safeguarding of water.
4   Water has economic value in all its competing uses and should be recognized as an economic good.

Barriers to climate adaptation in developing communities

However, in developing communities, many barriers exist in the practice of these four principles. Institutional barriers, knowledge gaps and gender bias, financing, and uncertainty are the main components preventing the deployment of effective adaptive water strategies.[82] In developing communities, local government officials who have the capability to promote change are limited by resources, training, and time.[83] There is a lack of trust, good governance, and political correlation between water and climate change. Community participation and knowledge of global warming is necessary for an adaptive water strategy, and if uncertainty of the impacts remains, it is more difficult to channel energy and finances in the needed areas.[84]

In order to overcome these barriers, the *Policy Brief* by the Cluster Group in Climate, Water, and Vulnerability hosted by the Swedish Water House created a list of recommendations for successful climate adaptation, despite present obstacles. These include promoting the IWRM principles, incorporating National Adaptation Programs for Action (NAPAs), encouraging stakeholder participation, gaining fresh and flexible funding for investment in water management, and ensuring that mechanisms that protect and promote human rights are in place.[85] By promoting integrated water resources management as well as making NAPAs cross-boundary, climate adaptation in developing communities is feasible. It is also vital to develop trust and maintain local participation in adaptive strategies.[86]

Climate adaptation must incorporate social and ecological efforts. Some solutions are "hard" in nature, while others are "soft." An example of a "hard" climate adaptation solution is implementing new or modifying old water infrastructure. Gaining local support and awareness is considered a "soft" solution, as it indirectly improves water management strategies.

Both solutions are crucial for climate adaptation strategies, and we must begin implementing water stewardship programs in order to increase resilience and decrease vulnerability to climate change. As climate change impacts our environment, infrastructure, and power generation, it will affect societal habits and economic behavior. Therefore, the adaptation strategies discussed in this chapter can provide more options for the future, even in uncertain conditions.

Innovation

Innovation is a much-used word these days. It is often used in the private sector and increasingly embraced by the public sector to address complex challenges such as education, healthcare, etc. Certainly, solutions to the energy–water–food Nexus challenge warrant innovative approaches to energy, water, and food: both as individual resource challenges but most importantly when viewed (as they should be) as a Nexus challenge.

Innovation platforms

The energy, water, and food Nexus is a "wicked problem." Tom Higley, a friend of Will's, entrepreneur, and founder of 10.10.10. net, asked if water was a "wicked problem." This question launched me on this view that wicked problems could not (likely) be solved by the "usual suspects." Speaking for myself (Will) I am in this category. I am a water practitioner and routinely attend water, Nexus, and technology innovation conferences – typically the same attendees with the same issues and, unfortunately, the same toolbox.

The Nexus is a wicked problem and wicked problems have a specific definition. Here are the characteristics of a wicked problem as defined by the Australian Public Service Commission Report:[87]

- Wicked problems are difficult to clearly define.
- Wicked problems have many interdependencies and are often multi-causal.
- Attempts to address wicked problems often lead to unforeseen consequences.
- Wicked problems are often not stable.
- Wicked problems usually have no clear solution.
- Wicked problems are socially complex.
- Wicked problems hardly ever sit conveniently within the responsibility of any one organization.
- Wicked problems involve changing behavior.
- Some wicked problems are characterized by chronic policy failure.

In particular, public policy innovation to address Nexus stress is ripe for new approaches to develop solutions. One new approach is 10.10.10 (101010.net). 10.10.10 refers to an organization with a program that addresses "10 wicked problems, 10 entrepreneurs for 10 days."

Tom and the team at 10.10.10 believe "The talents of today's best entrepreneurs are squandered." To quote 10.10.10 (our emphasis added):

The world doesn't need its best and brightest to build yet another app. We need them to grapple with wicked problems – the sprawling, intractable issues that must be tamed if we're going to build a better world. We need them to persuade investors to fund this vision. We need them to deliver these new products and services to a hungry and waiting market that will create and sustain new businesses and offer incentives for the creation of more things that deliver return on investment and benefit to the community, society and the world.

Whether they relate to health, *water, food, energy,* learning, infrastructure, waste or other areas, these are the problems too often left to governments, nonprofits and industrial giants. Why?

Because wicked problems present tremendous business opportunities, we realized we could engage entrepreneurs, investors and the market itself to confront them. But this can only be done with the right combination of entrepreneurial energy and insight. 10.10.10 harnesses this power and points it in the right direction. Prospective CEOs participate in 10.10.10 with the determination to build successful companies that attack wicked problems with market-based solutions.

Our interview with Tom Higley provides greater insight on the process and value creation.

Tom Higley is founder and CEO of 10.10.10, a nonprofit organization and program that connects entrepreneurs with validators (organizations with first-hand knowledge of "wicked problems" – those that are difficult or impossible to solve – and their possible solutions) to create fundable companies. The term "wicked problem" entered the academic lexicon via a 1973 paper by Horst W.J. Rittel and Melvin M. Webber, *Dilemmas in a General Theory of Planning*.[88]

Specifically, 10.10.10 invites 10 prospective CEOs from around the United States, each of them looking for his or her next big thing, to come together for 10 days to work on 10 wicked problems in areas like health, water, food, energy, learning, infrastructure, waste, security, and climate change.

The first 10.10.10 (10.10.10 Health) focused on wicked problems in health. It ran for 10 days (+1) in February 2015 and has already produced two funded companies providing health data solutions: BurstIQ, which uses blockchain technology to deliver secure data for care, for health, and for life; and Apostrophe Health, which works with over 20 employers across rural Colorado and the Front Rage to bring big company health benefits to self-insured employers of any size.

Tell us about your work in gaining momentum from the entrepreneurial community addressing the wicked problems that no single alignment is able to address. How did it come about, how is it working, what was some of the thinking behind it?

I'd highlight two significant areas of challenge on which we focus. The first of these challenges are the wicked problems in health, water, food, energy, learning, etc., that persist despite the best intentions and efforts of government, large industry, and academic institutions.

The second challenge concerns the world's serial entrepreneurs, who are not currently doing what they could or should to develop solutions to problems that matter. Together these two challenges serve as the core of 10.10.10 and its programs. 10.10.10 is focused on "complex adaptive systems" and the wicked problems that live within those systems, and is focused on the best way to engage and support serial entrepreneurs who plan to start new ventures.

Define "complex adaptive systems."

Complex adaptive systems may be organisms, they may be businesses, they may be economies, they may be political entities or structures. Cities, for example, are complex adaptive systems. Healthcare is a complex adaptive system, and so are all the other areas that we care about: health, water, food, energy, learning, infrastructure, waste, security, and climate change.

Complex adaptive systems are resistant to change in some ways, and *resilient* in others. They respond to changes in the environment through adaptation. But they actually *lock in* the wicked problems that government and large industry and research institutions can't address themselves. The systems themselves create certain incentives and reinforce certain dynamics in a way that ensures the persistence of these wicked problems.

Complex adaptive systems are resistant to change, but yet they're "adaptive?"

"Adaptive" means that these systems adapt to stimuli, to changes in the environment that occur from time to time. The system adapts in a way that supports its survival. Think of the system itself as comprised of autonomous agents, each acting according to common rules about how they should behave, what they should do next: like swarms of bees or huge flocks of birds – e.g., the Vaux's swifts in Portland Oregon deciding collectively, in an instant of time, to race down the chimney at Chapman Elementary School every year. In complex adaptive systems, this capacity to adapt both preserves the system *and locks in the wicked problems.*

How does this approach to solving wicked problems using complex adaptive systems open the eyes of those in large organizations to embracing fundamental change?

Large organizations and institutions have a greatly diminished capacity to move at speed, to focus on a particular issue or approach. Still, they well understand that innovation is a double-edged sword with the potential to help the large organization succeed. Or the potential to kill it. A Medallion Cab company in New York City with a lock on the taxi business might grow pretty comfortable, pretty set in its ways. But when an Uber or Lyft comes along with a completely different model for delivering a comparable service, the potential to upend the taxicab industry and destroy your business becomes all too obvious. As an established business, you might do better if you were more prepared. If you took advantage of the opportunity to peer a little bit into the future, you'd catch a glimpse of what new things technology and business model innovation are making possible.

If you are a large organization, you care deeply about this. Look at DEC, Kodak, Nokia, and Motorola. When the smartphone comes along, it doesn't matter if you currently *own the market* for flip phones. None of that matters if it becomes possible for someone to use what they've developed as a way to utterly disrupt and upend the industry in which you function. This is what entrepreneurs have great potential to do. Large organizations and institutions have every reason to *care* but they have little internal capacity to *protect* themselves against potential disruption. So these organizations are beginning to understand that the limitless potential, the true benefit of innovation, comes to the large organization that ventures outside its own walls.

In the US more than 80 percent of our energy supply still comes from coal, gas, and nuclear power plants. But wind and solar energy now costs less than fossil fuels in 30 countries. Just a few years from now two-thirds of the rest of the world's nations are expected to join them. Given this situation, and the speed with which entrepreneurs can move, the large organizations that will survive and flourish will be those that get close enough to the innovation occurring outside their walls to see a new future.

Large organizations want to do it themselves, but can't? By nature of their DNA?

Large organizations are required by their size and scale to operate on a more *incremental* basis. Those within large organizations who appreciate the power of innovation often imagine that because their large organizations are resource-rich, they can aspire to the same things that entrepreneurs do. But this rarely happens.

If your business is successful and well established, if you are generating substantial revenue, you cannot afford to ignore your current customers. This is Clay Christensen's classic and still powerful insight from *Innovators Dilemma*. What may be tomorrow's biggest market opportunity is still, today, almost certainly too small to justify a large organization giving it any focus or attention. Consequently, internal efforts to turn a large organization's attention to future, speculative opportunities will meet with substantial resistance.

Many companies address this issue through acquisition. They keep close tabs on early-stage companies that have begun to secure traction in a particular market space and acquire any company that has developed innovations that will support the larger organization's products, services, or lines of business.

Think about the largest companies and most successful companies on the planet today, those that have been created in, let's say, the last 15 years: Google, Facebook, Amazon. A generation earlier, that would include Apple and Microsoft. Not one of these companies began as part of a larger company. None of these large extraordinarily successful companies will have, as their point of origin, the innovation initiative that takes place within a larger company. That's not where they will begin. They can't begin there.

When I talk about "venturing outside your walls" I mean using something like a 10.10.10 to begin to see, out there in the wild, what's *happening* – where the potential lies. When you do this as a large organization, you protect yourself against what might happen if you fail to see or pay attention to the phenomenon of disruptive market evolution. This is why you have substantial incentive within a large organization to secure a ringside seat to the innovation process undertaken by successful serial entrepreneurs. When you have a seat at the table, you *also* have an incentive to put important problems on the table – problems your organization wants solutions for but just cannot afford to solve itself.

This is what we do at 10.10.10. We offer large organizations a seat at the table. And in addition to supplying problems that matter, these organizations help validate possible solutions. Instead of acquiring a company that built a working solution based on the wrong standards or models or approaches, you can – as a larger company – offer meaningful input before a product or service is developed.

And there's another benefit. If a startup is working on a problem that matters to you, you can support the effort *without* having to explain why you allocated substantial internal resources to an effort that fails to get the green light for further development and commercialization. If the startup fails, it fails outside your walls. You've dodged a bullet. And what you learn from its failure may well be worth any cost you incur by supporting the process. On the other hand, if it begins to succeed you will see this well ahead of most of the other players in your market. You can then decide whether to gain further market advantage by investing in, partnering with, or acquiring the startup.

So, wicked problems are at the heart of it? And entrepreneurial thinking is the solution?

Yes and no. Developing an effective solution has required much more than "entrepreneurial thinking." The first thing we do, among many others, that is really designed to begin to address wicked problems, is to bring successful entrepreneurs together. These entrepreneurs are not beholden to "the system." They think, live and operate outside the realm within which wicked problems fester and persist. And because these entrepreneurs are less dependent on system, they are willing and able to disrupt it. They are also prepared to secure private sector capital to fund the solutions that are necessary. They are, in effect, outsiders who know how to make things happen.

Are you the matchmaker? What is that process like?

I suppose we are, in some a sense, a kind of matchmaker. But it may be more accurate to see us as creating a program and establishing a process and context for breakthrough innovation to occur. Diversity plays a critical role: sector diversity; geographic diversity; gender diversity; ethnic diversity; cultural diversity. When we focus on wicked problems in a particular area – for example, in health, water, food, or energy – we look for people who bring a background and experience developed outside the domain. We look for people with tech experience, people with success in other sectors. This ensures that our program encourages an outsider's perspective and understanding. Outsiders don't see problems in the same way industry insiders do. 10.10.10 creates a kind of "wormhole" that connects the entrepreneurial culture (its language, culture, and perspective) with the large organization and institution (and its respective universe, culture, and perspective).

The culture that supports entrepreneurs and startups is real and quite distinct. It has its own vocabulary. Its own dress code. It has an understanding, a perspective, about what things matter and which outcomes are good. Similarly, the culture in large organizations and institutions have their own vocabularies and dress codes, their own notions about how to talk about and think about these problems, their own notions about which outcomes are good.

These two very different cultures, the entrepreneurial culture and the culture that includes large organizations and established institutions, do not often interact or intersect.

They do not attend one another's gatherings, conferences, seminars, events, or parties. On the rare occasion when an executive from a large organization attends a startup or entrepreneurial gathering, she can feel ill at ease or out of place. So the wormhole we provide facilitates connections among those who have very different perspectives.

Those different perspectives create what might be described as *edges* or boundaries and these edges consist of the collision and interaction sparked by these different perspectives. This is where the magic happens. There is a little less magic where people are the same, think in the same way and talk in the same ways. Breakthroughs happen when *divergent* attitudes, perspectives, and understandings prompt new ways of thinking and acting. This context allows differences to surface in good ways and support extraordinary outcomes.

What does entrepreneurial thinking have to offer the large organizational model?

Value exists for each player, from small to large, arrayed along continuum – with speed and focus on the X axis and size and scale on the Y axis. The entrepreneur – not the young company or start-up with a founding team already in place, but the lone entrepreneur who plans to start a new venture – this entrepreneur moves at *light speed.* He or she is extraordinary focused. As a group, they make rapid decisions. They may pivot 50, 60, 70 times – exploring, rejecting, and revamping different ways to address a specific problem, address a different market segment, develop a new solution, explore ways to generate and capture value, or discover ways to create an "unfair" advantage. And they may do all of this in a space *of a few days.*

Large companies cannot do this. Large organizations and institutions operate at scale. They have proven business models, established customers, substantial resources, networks of relationships, channel partners, suppliers, a host of understandings and learnings that are extremely valuable. What *we* do is this: we bring together the entrepreneur – including the value that come from speed, focus, and extensive experience

starting new ventures – and we combine this with the extraordinary capabilities of large organizations, institutions and
even governmental entities. This facilitates an unprecedented
exchange – about the problems that matter, ideas for addressing these problems, information that will be important in
creating a new venture and the value that can be created,
delivered, and captured.

**Is financing at the heart of these collaborations? Is it always all
about money or are there higher ideals in place?**

In 10.10.10's case there is a clear, designed approach to developing solutions that include ROI – a return on investment.
Our focus on market-based solutions is important because it
ensures access to capital – the fuel that innovation requires.
So, yes, there is certainly a financial aspect to any outcome
that we would count as successful. However, there is also a
critical *impact* component for any outcome that we count as
successful. In other words, we will never be satisfied with ROI
alone. It is *not* "all about the money."

Let me use an illustration. Think of a bow tie. Think of the
knot in the bow tie as that moment in time when a new venture is created. The things that live to the *right* side of the bow
tie are things that have been in focus for the last 10 or so years
in the world of startups. All the things that new ventures do
live on the right side of the bow tie, things that happen only
after a new venture has been formed and funded. These are
things like "customer discovery," "minimum viable product,"
"product market fit," growing a customer base, raising Series
A or Series B capital, etc. Similarly Y Combinator, the accel-
erator in the Bay Area that has done so phenomenally well,
and TechStars, which began in Boulder in 2006 and has now
expanded throughout the world, these organizations, widely
known as "accelerators," live on the right side of the bow tie.

Until recently, there hasn't been a *left* side of the bow tie.
There have been amorphous and unclear notions about how
a new venture should come together, about how a founder
ought to think about working with other co-founders to start

a venture, usually starting with an "idea." It is possible that most entrepreneurial ventures in the modern age have followed this model.

If you frame the left side of the bow tie in terms of a new venture that starts with an idea, it becomes natural for the right side of the bow tie to be all about "exits" and "liquidity" – to be "all about the money." Alternatively, we think about the *left* side of the bow tie as an entirely different way to start new ventures. We begin a collection of *problems* that matter (vs. ideas), and each entrepreneur distills this list of problems to *the single problem on which he or she will focus their new business.* We begin by challenging each founder to assess problem or "founder problem fit" or "founder opportunity fit." The process then focuses on framing how the founder should go about identifying the best opportunities and identifying and mitigating risk.

So the left side of the bow tie starts with a collection of problems, possibilities, and opportunities, and through the process these are *distilled* to a single problem, a singular point of focus. The entrepreneur explores sources of "unfair" advantage that might be available, an advantage that could be about technology, intellectual property, access to data, distribution, or regulatory/policy change – something that gives the entrepreneur a defensible reason to believe success in the marketplace can be achieved. All of this lives on the left side of the bow tie – an entire process that informs your understanding of opportunity and risk and your decision-making well before you start your new venture.

So this approach puts you in a different place. You're not only thinking about it as an outcome, the idea of an exit, or liquidity, but about whether you solved a wicked problem – a problem that really matters to you and to the world. The solution to wicked problems is where impact lives. So the end game starts to be not just about return on investment, not just about money but how you solve the wicked problem related to health or water, or food or energy, or learning. It starts to be about the impact that you're generating because you've addressed that wicked problem with a sustainable, market-based solution.

What is it about the large organization that brings them to the table in the first place?

They are scared to death. If you're a C-suite executive in some of these organizations you very well understand that your days – and those of your organization – may be numbered.

The other thing is, large organizations aren't stupid; they aren't necessarily bad at what they do. They don't perform poorly in the speed and focus dimension because they're *inept*. They perform badly in those dimensions because when they reach a certain size they have many more variables they have to think about and take into account. And they have many, many more aspects of the communication process, reconciling divergent perspectives, within the organization itself and across the industry, so they can't focus in the same way. They can't move at the same speed. And in fact when an organization of size tries to do that, they hurt the organization. They hurt its core business. So hyper-speed and hyper-focus – the thing that entrepreneurs do so very well – doesn't work for a large organization. It's dangerous for them. This is why they seek a seat at the table. They are savvy enough to seek opportunities to leverage entrepreneurs who *can* operate with hyper-speed and focus, to externalize innovation initiatives that represent both opportunity and risk to the core business.

How do we project this into the idea of the water–energy–food Nexus right now? That's a wicked problem. Where you see some lights at the end of the tunnel?

So we can't say what the lights come from, what they look like. We can't describe them yet. What we can describe at the moment is program and process to begin to surface the complex adaptive system and the intertwined elements and components that have to be taken into consideration as you're exploring a particular market-based solution. So the water–energy–food Nexus is fascinating because what is happening there is also happening in the other sectors I've described – health, learning, infrastructure, waste, security, etc.

What are you seeing as the obstacles to solutions in this complex instance of the Nexus?

You cannot talk about food without an understanding how water quality and supply are measured, assessed, and assured. And when we talk about energy – its source, its cost, its sustainability, its method of distribution – the implications for food and water become immediately apparent. We have to begin to incorporate in our thinking and in our approach models that recognize these seemingly disparate elements as operating in a dynamic relationship with one another. And this dynamic relationship, generally speaking, isn't something people think about.

Often when people think in business terms, it is easy to think "if I do A, with B as the result, I could get to C." It's a straight-line calculation. But resources like food, energy, and water – and problems related to them – do not lend themselves to linear models. The complexity in each area is often compounded when an approach taken in one area yields unanticipated and unintended effects in another. We have to begin to understand how the system *as a whole* works and behaves. We need to give thought to the sensitivity of the system to specific inputs.

When I think about A to get to B and from B to C, I'm thinking about an easy and simplified path, but the problems we are describing here, problems that are part of the water–energy–food Nexus, this set of problems isn't like that. This takes us back to the notion of complexity and complexity theory. Complex adaptive systems can be characterized by common elements: individual agents following simple rules generate complex outcomes. The system has identifiable feedback loops, it has sensitivity to initial conditions, and the interactions of agents generate emergent behavior. If the system elements are altered or disrupted, the system will adapt or react.

Complexity and complexity theory began to come into its own perhaps 40 years ago, which still makes it a relative newcomer. The Santa Fe Institute, founded in 1984, is probably the best-known institution focusing on complexity theory and science, but the history of complexity dates back to Henri Poincaré and his work on the "three body problem." The path forward from Poincaré extends through Edward Lorenz, and his interest in weather and the nonlinear "chaos" he observed.

I'll call attention to two notable books: James Gleick's *Chaos: Making a New Science* and Geoffrey West's recent work *Scale: The Universal Laws of Growth, Innovation, Sustainability, and the Pace of Life in Organisms, Cities, Economies, and Companies.* Gleick's book put chaos theory and complexity on the map in terms of the general public. And in his book, Geoffrey West, a theoretical physicist who was president of the Santa Fe Institute from 2005–2009, talks about powerfully interconnected elements, which is a good place to begin seeing and thinking about these things. Geoffrey, a pioneer in the field of complexity, offers a new way of thinking and talking about complexity, scale, and the way different systems behave. These new perspectives are beginning to capture the attention of entrepreneurs and investors who appreciate what may be at stake for humans, companies, economies, and cities.

Regarding the Nexus, the city context is important. We have begun to hear this frequently: in the previous century less than 10 percent of the world's population was living in cities. Today 50 percent of the world's population lives in cities. In 20 years, two thirds of the world's population will be living in cities. By the mid-century 75 percent of the world's population will live in cities. This means that impact on people, on organizations, on institutions, and regions will be felt in the context of cities, and the work to be done to address this problem will need to focus on *cities.*

In cities complexity issues come into play in an even more interesting way. Cities are, themselves, extraordinarily complex adaptive systems. How should cities think about the water–energy–food Nexus? Can a city of any substantial size anywhere in the world afford to ignore the questions posed by water risk, water supply, and water quality, and the implication these questions have for food availability and cost? Can the energy and water required to maintain the supply of food for rapidly growing cities be left out of the calculus? How does a shift to renewables impact food prices and the cost to supply water? Will innovation and greater efficiency in agricultural uses of water lead to unintended consequences – e.g., greater consumptive use?

How does 10.10.10 or any other facilitator make the solution magic happen?

At 10.10.10 we don't disclose the problems to the invited entrepreneurs ahead of time. They arrive, and on the first day they attend a "big reveal" in which each problem is pitched to the CEOs and to the assembled community. The point here is to treat these start-up CEOs like "investors." While they often don't fully understand this themselves, they will be investing the next chapter of their lives in their new venture. They have good reason to do substantial due diligence. That's what the process on the left side of the bow tie is all about. This is why we begin our program by having 10 "problem advocates" deliver "pitches" for each of the wicked problems. And each problem advocate pitch follows a basic format: (1) the problem; (2) the pain caused by the problem; (3) the impacted persons or groups; (4) the reason an entrepreneur could now succeed with a market-based solution; and (5) encouragement to choose *this* problem (and ignore the other nine).

Where do the problems come from?

They almost surely have come from extensive conversations with people in large organizations and institutions, people who have seen or become aware of these wicked problems but know their organizations are ill-equipped to solve the problems themselves. They contribute the problems, and they contribute to an understanding of the sector in which the problems live, and they contribute their understandings about how best to explore market-based solutions. Some approaches to addressing these problems *won't* be interesting in the marketplace; others will.

So these large organizations have plenty of incentive to be at the table and the entrepreneurs, for their part, they have huge incentives to participate. They can't possibly process this much information this quickly any other way. Past participants have described the program as "the most powerful experience of my professional life." And some have said that through the program and process they were able to accomplish in six months what would previously have taken them years to do.

Step us through a timeline in the 10.10.10 program. How do you cover so much relevant ground in so short a timeframe?

The first thing that happens in the 10.10.10 context is intense focus on the problems themselves. You see four to five days of really unpacking research that has been done for months in advance about these problems that is available to the entrepreneurs, validators, and what we call ninjas, people who are kind of a founding an ad hoc founding team. And this is where it gets interesting.

After four or so days of this the next step in the process is the formation of 10 "sprint teams," where a Google venture-style sprint drives a process, and the process is about understanding that you're going to create a *testable prototype* by the end of the five days.

So Day One is about mapping what's possible. Day Two is about sketching what you're going to do or build. Day Three is about making key decisions, connected to the prototype you'll create. Day Four is creating the prototype itself, and Day Five is testing the prototype.

And the validators – companies, NGOs, foundations, and others with first-hand knowledge of wicked problems and those working on solutions – all play an important part at the beginning of the process, helping to frame what is important and what that conversation should look like. But the *perspective* is what drives the entrepreneurs. They make the decisions about what happens in those sprints.

At the end of the process, these validators are actually there to talk about and engage in that test related to the prototype, so they get to see what happens. That's how this process comes together, and of course 10 days isn't a good timeframe to be thinking about starting new ventures. It's a great timeframe to *think about* where you *might* look to start a new venture. It's really over the next nine months that 10.10.10 expects its CEOs to develop or create the new ventures.

How does this thinking apply in the context of solving issues facing water and its interaction with food and energy?

For 10.10.10 Health, we have been supported by the Colorado Health Foundation and key validators, including Kaiser Permanente, the American Diabetes Association, the Medical Group Management Association, US Health and Human Services, and many others. For our upcoming 10.10.10 Cities program focused on water and infrastructure, we are supported by the Walton Family Foundation and the Gates Family Foundation. They are both funders and validators. They understand something about the problems and the stakeholders. We expect to have the City and County of Denver, Denver Water, Tap-In, the Greenway Foundation, Water for People, Imagine H2O, and many others in a Denver program.

Key officials, organizations, and institutions understand better than most entrepreneurs how water is delivered and how water quality and supply may vary in response to key inputs. By bringing these folks to the table we combine technology, intellectual property, market knowledge, and operational insight – perspectives that when taken together may surface new opportunities that haven't yet found their way into the marketplace.

What are some of the other components that are relevant to this incredible aspiration to sew these three foundations of culture – energy, water, and food – together as far as changing thinking?

One critical component is *data*. You don't want to function in the realm of opinion and intuition alone. You want to make sure that you have good visibility into what's happening in the real world, and that's not just about static information. It is about flows – a key concept in systems thinking.

You need to be able to see what has changed at what time. You want local data, but you also need access to regional, national, and even global data. We know, we understand that the actors and key stakeholders are interdependent and interconnected. Things that happen in one part of the world influence things in another part of the world. (The title of Edward Lorenz's seminal 1972 paper helps illustrate the point: *Does the Flap of a Butterfly's Wings in Brazil Set Off a Tornado in Texas?*)

And how do you create a mindset that opens up the possibilities as to the influences from outside the immediate frame of reference?

Yaneer Bar-Yam, author of *Making Things Work*, is an influential complexity theorist. Thinking and reasoning from a complexity perspective, he posits a connection between several things that many do not think are connected. For example, his work on the causes of the global food crisis has been cited by *Wired* magazine among the top 10 scientific discoveries of 2011.

In this work he suggests that a big surge in food prices in 2007 and 2008 followed by another dramatic increase in food prices in 2011 were precipitated by policy decisions in the United States related to corn, ethanol, and the deregulation of commodities market. When taken together, these policy decisions led to higher global food prices – a doubling of food prices around the world. US deregulation of commodities markets and the mortgage crisis left capital with no place to go. It flowed into the commodities markets triggering substantial increases in food prices. Bar-Yam and his co-authors say these price increases triggered global social unrest that resulted in the so-called "Arab Spring." As food prices rose in the Middle East rose, we soon saw riots in the streets. The combination of what happened with food prices and what happened with the mortgage crisis contributed to the set of conditions that made the Arab Spring and its aftermath a reality. This fascinating example of interconnectedness and complexity helps illustrate the need to consider the water–energy–food Nexus from a systems perspective.

This brings us back to the diversity I mentioned earlier. Having a common frame of reference, a shared point of view, isn't a bad thing. It helps us work effectively and efficiently. But a common frame of reference can become problematic if it isn't also accompanied by an awareness of the existence of *other* frames of reference, other perspectives. 10.10.10's "wormhole" puts these alternative points of view, and the people who share them, front and center.

In June of 2017 I (Will) attended 10.10.10 Health and at the midpoint of the program Tom talked about 10.10.10 Cities. He showed the following slide (with a slight modification) to illustrate the relationship between entrepreneurs, multinationals, and the public sector. His key point is that all of these stakeholders have unique attributes that *collectively can solve wicked problems.*

Entrepreneurs have the speed and focus to address environmental and social problems. Many of these entrepreneurs hold the view that failing fast and forward is designed to develop solutions that can be scaled to address a particular problem. Processes such as an innovation sprint are designed to rapidly identify potential solutions to problems.[89]

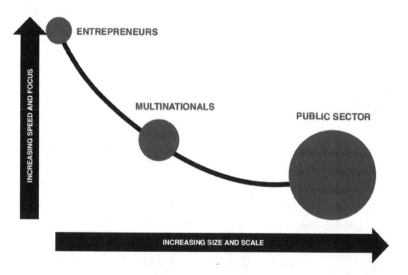

Figure 4.3 **Innovation: entrepreneurs, multinationals, and the public sector**

Source: T. Higley, 10.10.10 Founders LLC, 2017.

How do we harness this speed and focus with the know-how and scale of multinationals *and* the potential scale and impact of the public sector? How do we even connect entrepreneurs, multinationals, and the public sector? Building programs such as 10.10.10 is a unique way.

Prize competitions, incentives, and green bonds

Increasingly, innovative approaches to either drive public policy changes or catalyze change are coming from prize competitions, incentives, and alternative funding tools such as green bonds.

In a world where public funding for programs is scarce, alternative approaches to address the energy–water–food Nexus challenges are essential.

Prize competitions

While taking a different approach, prize competitions, are also showing up to address the need to accelerate innovation in public policy innovation. One such recent prize competition was launched by ImagineH2O[90] to tackle innovation in California public water.[91] While this competition was focused on water prize, competitions can be crafted to focus on public policy and Nexus challenges. First a bit about the ImagineH2O competition.

According to Michael Kiparsky from the Center for Law, Energy & the Environment (CLEE) at UC Berkeley School of Law, and Richard Roos-Collins of the Water and Power Law Group (WPLG), "Imagine H2O's Policy Program identifies and supports policies leading to the broader adoption of water innovation in the California market and beyond."[92] The rationale for the California Water Policy Challenge is provided below:

Data is essential to help California's farmers, businesses and communities monitor and manage water resources more effectively. Promising data solutions exist, but policy barriers prevent their adoption in municipal, agricultural and industrial markets. A supportive policy environment is vital to foster a market for water innovation.

IH2O's second annual California Water Policy Challenge aimed to strengthen the quality of water management by accelerating the development of water data innovations and technologies.

Their innovative idea is that:

California law requires that water rights be put to reasonable and beneficial use. Effective administration of this require-ment depends on an information system that includes all water rights and their terms. Such a system doesn't exist. Currently, legal records pertaining to this precious resource are housed as 10 million pages of paper files at the State Water Resources Control Board (SWRCB). The records are not indexed for search by author, date, or topics, and records for pre-1914 water rights are scattered throughout 58 county courthouses and other repositories. Thus, the SWRCB and stakeholders cannot effectively review legal records necessary to evaluate relative priorities among water rights in a given watershed, to resolve conflicts or to manage shortages. Further, SB 88 ena-bles the SWRCB to require real-time reporting of water use and diversion data by water users but will only enforce this requirement if it is able to assimilate and analyze the data col-lected. An accurate accounting of water rights will empower more effective and sustainable management of statewide water resources. The proposed water information system is the ena-bling capacity necessary for enforcement of SB 88, permitting decision-making informed by real-time data in an era in which California frequently faces systemic shortages and conflicts.

Build a modern information system of water rights and water use that will enable deliberate, real-time decision-making on the allocation of water in California.

The other winners were:

- *Mammoth Trading:* Incentivize the agricultural community to participate in groundwater data collection through the development of innovative groundwater markets.

- *Got Produce:* Improve access to loans for innovative water efficiency technologies for farmers through third-party validation of water savings.
- *Water in the West at Stanford University:* Build a flexible digital tool that quantifies the environmental, economic, and social benefits and risks of green infrastructure (GI) projects to support increased integration with urban planning projects.

Imagine using prize competitions such as ImagineH2O and entrepreneurial platforms such as 10.10.10 to drive innovation in public policy at the energy–water–food Nexus. We could capture the innovative ideas of a diverse group of global stakeholders to tackle this challenge with a fresh point of view.

Prize competitions work for innovation in technology, why not for public policy?

Incentives: conservation synergy

In addition to prize competitions, "conservation synergy" can also address Nexus challenges. A conservation strategy spanning two or more resource categories can change behavior, with a resultant conservation in resources.

The energy and water utility sectors are intertwined – water is used for energy production and energy is used for water extraction and treatment. This is a logical place for policy to promote conservation of both resources. Fortunately, there are examples where utilities have partnered to promote conservation incentives to the benefit of both.

"Conservation synergy" has gained traction as an innovative approach to reducing energy and water use. In the 2013 report, *Conservation Synergy – The Case for Integrating Water and Energy Efficiency Programs* by the Western Resource Advocates (WRA),[93] the authors conclude that joint efficiency programs between energy and water utilities are a good business decision. These programs result in "higher participation rates, increased customer satisfaction, coordinated and complementary program design, and an improved reputation for working smarter – not harder."

The process mapped out by the WRA brings together senior management and staff from regulatory bodies to conduct market analyses, identify the best opportunities for collaboration as well as the costs, benefits, risks, and financing options for projects, then obtain regulatory approval, conduct the projects, and then repeat the cycle. A few case studies from the WRA report are provided below.[94]

- *Joint rebates.* In 2008, the investor-owned, California-based utility PG&E, along with several water agencies in California, offered a rebate program for high-efficiency clothes washers. The rebate in 2013 ranged from $100 to $125 – this includes a $50 rebate from PG&E and a variable rebate from $50 to $75 from the water utility. PG&E has seen a 63 percent increase in customer participation since the water utilities joined the program and the water utilities have seen a 30 percent increase in their customer participation. The program has since expanded to 41 water agencies (municipal, regional, and private utilities).

- *Joint audits.* Three Texas utilities – Austin Water Utility, Texas Gas Service, and Austin Energy — collaborated in 2011 to develop a "Multifamily Energy and Water Efficiency Program." The program, funded in part by the US Department of Energy, is designed to conserve water, electricity, and gas. The program provides resource efficiency improvements for multifamily residential dwellings and is projected to upgrade approximately 1,900 multifamily units, resulting in approximately 4.7 million kilowatt-hours of energy savings and 10 million gallons of water. One of the key innovations is that the program overcomes the "split incentive" problem, where the property owner incurs the cost of the upgrade but the renter earns the resource-efficiency benefits. The holistic approach to resource efficiency created enough benefit to the owners for them to participate in the program and overcome the split incentive problem.

- *Joint building efficiency upgrades.* The Los Angeles Department of Water and Power (LADWP – a municipal utility) and the Southern California Gas company (SoCalGas – an investor-owned utility) launched six residential and commercial energy–water programs in late 2012. This collaboration made available to utility customers several resource-efficiency programs concurrently, including a retro commissioning program to tune up non-residential building equipment, a program to implement energy and water efficiency projects for residential and small business facilities, and energy efficiency upgrades for the Los Angeles Unified School District.

While not numerous, these programs quantify the tangible value in coordinated energy and water efficiency programs. Now, if we could combine these types of incentive programs with agriculture we would have a transformative Nexus solution.

Why don't we have more joint incentive programs? These programs make sense and the value can be quantified. A study by the Oakland, California-based Pacific Institute sheds light on the challenges that need to be overcome to scale these joint incentive programs.[95] The major barriers identified by the study conducted by the Pacific Institute are:

- The water sector has limited or inconsistent funding available to invest in combined programs;
- It has limited staff time;
- There is insufficient guidance about how to equitably allocate costs and benefits among project partners;
- Water-related pricing policies (e.g., few mechanisms for cost-recovery and concerns about revenue stability) are problematic;
- The is a lack of an established relationship between potential water and energy partners.

Other barriers include "fragmentation within and across sectors, a lack of appetite for innovation and risk-taking within the water sector, a lack of directive from regulatory agencies, and a lack of awareness about water–energy connections at the utility level."[96]

What does success look like with these programs? Both WRA and the Pacific Institute report that successful programs managed to address the following challenges:

- Obtaining funding from multiple sources;
- Offering customers new or expanded services at lower time and money costs than would have been required to implement such programs individually;
- Utilizing a third party to administer the program;
- Demonstrating the value in connecting efficiency programs – that saving water saves energy.

Green bonds

Alternative approaches to funding centralized public water infrastructure projects have emerged. In particular, in the US, where there is aging infrastructure coupled with a persistent lack of public funds, several high visibility green bond projects have spawned. The movement has in part been catalyzed by the UK-based Climate Bonds Initiative,[97] which is "an international, investor-focused not-for-profit. It's the only organization in the world focusing on mobilizing the US$100 trillion bond market for climate change solutions."

The Climate Bonds Initiative developed criteria for water investments that can be used to back green bonds and climate bonds certified under the Climate Bond Standard. The group developed criteria for water-related investments in the areas of "clean water projects, water treatment infrastructure, agricultural usage, storm and flood drainage and protection."

Likely the most prominent example of the structure and impact of a green bond for water is with the DC Water and Sewer Authority (DC Water). In 2014, DC Water, Goldman Sachs, and the Calvert Foundation issued a green bond that was the US's first Environmental Impact Bond (EIB). In summary:[98]

- The green bond was issued to an initial green infrastructure project in its DC Clean Rivers Project, a US$2.6 billion program to control storm water runoff and improve the District's water quality, creating a healthier future for District residents. This deal offers a new type of financial instrument to fund environmental capital projects.

- The US$25 million, tax-exempt EIB was sold in a private placement to the Goldman Sachs Urban Investment Group and Calvert Foundation. The proceeds of the bond will be used to construct green infrastructure practices designed to mimic natural processes to absorb and slow surges of storm-water during periods of heavy rainfall, reducing the incidence and volume of combined sewer overflows (CSOs) that pollute the District's waterways. CSO reduction has become an increasingly urgent environmental challenge as a result of climate change, which has increased the frequency and severity of intense rainfall events.

- The EIB allows DC Water to attract investment in green infrastructure through an innovative financing technique whereby the costs of installation are paid for by DC Water, but the performance risk of the green infrastructure in managing storm water runoff is shared amongst DC Water and the investors. As a result, payments on the EIB may vary based on the proven success of the environmental intervention as measured by a rigorous evaluation. By financing this project through the EIB, DC Water seeks to create a model-funding mechanism that other municipalities can leverage to advance the use of green infrastructure to address storm water management in their communities.

- Both Goldman Sachs and Calvert also viewed this as innovation in infrastructure funding. "We're thrilled to partner with DC Water to help pioneer this innovative financing mechanism that will not only benefit the community environmentally, but also stimulate local job creation," said Margaret Anadu, Goldman Sachs Managing Director who leads the Urban Investment Group. "This first-ever environmental impact bond will finance the construction of green infrastructure and support economic development in the District."

- "Calvert Foundation is excited to test the efficacy of green infrastructure in the District," said Investments Director Beth Bafford. "This work is critical for residents in our hometown and has national implications for how to finance green infrastructure solutions to combat the effects of extreme weather on aged, vulnerable sewer systems."

In addition to the DC Water green bond, San Francisco Water Power Sewer also issued a water bond under the Climate Bonds Standard. The initial $240 million wastewater revenue bonds will be used for sustainable stormwater management projects.

Notes

1 Einstein, Albert, quoted on GoodReads.com, https://www.goodreads.com/quotes/7275-in-the-middle-of-difficulty-lies-opportunity, accessed November 12, 2017.

2 *The Telegraph,* "Jean-Claude Juncker's Most Outrageous Political Quotations," July 15, 2014.

3 Jamal Saghir, WRG team meeting, Stockholm, 2009.

4 2030 WRG, "Charting Our Water Future: Economic Frameworks to Inform Decision-Making," 2009.

5 Ibid.

6 2030 WRG, "2016 Annual Report."

7 2030 WRG, "2016 Annual Report."

8 2030 WRG, "2015 Annual Report: Moving Towards Implementation," 2016.

9 2030 WRG, Personal Communication

10 "Knowledge & Tools," 2030 WRG, https://www.2030wrg.org/knowledge-tools/, accessed September 20, 2017.

11 World Economic Forum, "Annual Meeting 2017 System Initiatives Programme," 2017.

12 "Knowledge & Tools," 2030 WRG, https://www.2030wrg.org/knowledge-tools/, accessed September 20, 2017.

13 Antoine de Saint-Exupéry, quoted on GoodReads.com, www.goodreads.com/quotes/87476-a-goal-without-a-plan-is-just-a-wish, accessed September 20, 2017.

14 United Nations, "United Nations Millennium Declaration," September 18, 2000.

15 "United Nations Millennium Development Goals," United Nations, www.un.org/millenniumgoals/, accessed September 20, 2017.

16 "Rain: Water for Africa," The Coca-Cola Company, www.coca-colacompany.com/rain, accessed September 20, 2017.

17 "MDG Momentum," United Nations, www.un.org/millenniumgoals/mdgmomentum.shtml, accessed September 20, 2017.

18 "Home Page," WHO/UNICEF JMP, https://www.wssinfo.org/, accessed September 20, 2017.

19 WHO, "Guidelines for Drinking-water Quality," 2008.

20 Kyle Onda, Joe LoBuglio, and Jamie Bartram, "Global Access to Safe Water: Accounting for Water Quality and the Resulting Impact on MDG Progress," *International Journal of Environmental Research and Public Health* 9, no. 3, March 2012: 880–894.

21 "The Water Crisis," water.org, http://water.org/water-crisis/water-sanitation-facts/, accessed September 20, 2017.

22 WaterAid America, "Annual report summary, 2015–16," 2016.

23 Allan H. Smith, Elena O. Lingas, and Mahfuzar Rahman, "Contamination of Drinking-Water by Arsenic in Bangladesh: A Public Health Emergency," *Bulletin of the World Health Organization* 78, no. 9, 2000: 1093–103.

24 "Goal 6 Targets," UN Development Programme, www.undp.org/content/undp/en/home/sustainable-development-goals/goal-6-clean-water-and-sanitation/targets/, accessed September 20, 2017.

25 Banega Swachh India, "80 Percent of World's Wastewater Discharged Untreated: UN," March 22, 2017.

26 Shafiqul Islam, "Hydropolitics of the Nile, the 18th Camel and Water Diplomacy," Water Diplomacy, February 7, 2014.

27 "Home Page", Millennium Challenge Corporation, https://www.mcc.gov/, accessed September 20, 2017.

28 Millennium Challenge Corporation, "MCC Partners With The Coca-Cola Africa Foundation to Expand Access to Clean Water," March 22, 2013.

29 "Rain: Water for Africa," The Coca-Cola Company.

30 Guy Hutton and Mili Varughese, "The Costs of Meeting the 2030 Sustainable Development Goal Targets on Drinking Water, Sanitation, and Hygiene," World Bank Group, January 2016.

31 Bill Gates, "How State Budgets Are Breaking Schools," TED Talk, March 2011.

32 "Water Stewardship and the United Nations Sustainable Development Goal 6: Ensure Access to Water and Sanitation for All," The Coca-Cola Company, www.coca-colacompany.com/stories/water-stewardship-and-the-united-nations-sustainable-development-goal-6-ensure-access-to-water-and-sanitation-for-all, accessed September 20, 2017.

33 "UN Global Goals for Sustainable Development," Unilever, https://www.unilever.com/sustainable-living/our-approach-to-reporting/un-global-goals-for-sustainable-development/, accessed September 20, 2017.

34 Sustainable Brands, "Nestlé, Tesco, Unilever CEOs Among 'Champions 12.3,' Determined to Halve Global Food Waste," January 22, 2016.

35 CEO Water Mandate, "Guide to Water-Related Collective Action," https://ceowatermandate.org/collectiveaction/, accessed September 20, 2017.

36 CEO Water Mandate, "The CEO Water Mandate: Guide to Responsible Business Engagement with Water Policy," November 15, 2010.

37 "The WASH at the Workplace Pledge," WBCSD, www.wbcsd.org/Clusters/Water/WASH-access-to-water-sanitation-and-hygiene/WASH-at-the-workplace-Pledge, accessed September 20, 2017.

38 "Deforestation Resolution," The Consumer Goods Forum, www.theconsumergoodsforum.com/sustainability-strategic-focus/sustainability-resolutions/deforestation-resolution, accessed September 20, 2017.

39 Mahmoud Mohieldin and Svetlana Klimenko, "The Private Sector and the SDGs," Project Syndicate, February 6, 2017.

40 United Nations, "UN, Private Sector to Create Platform for Financing SDGs," October 10, 2016.

41 OECD, "Policy Coherence for Sustainable Development in the SDG Framework: Shaping Targets and Monitoring Progress," 2015.

42 Ibid.

43 Ki-Moon, Ban, "Big Idea 2014: The Year for Climate Action," United Nations, December 2013, www.un.org/climatechange/summit/2013/12/big-idea-2014-the-year-for-climate-action-by-ban-ki-moon/, accessed November 12, 2017.

44 Testimony of Dr Peter H. Gleick, December 1st, 2010.

45 Josué Medellín-Azuara, et al., "Water Management Adaptation with Climate Change," California Climate Change Center, March 2009.

46 Ibid.

47 Ibid.

48 Ibid.

49 Ibid.

50 Ibid.

51 Ibid.

52 Ibid.

53 Matthews, J. H and Le Quesne, T. "Adapting Water Management: A Primer on Coping with Climate Change," WWF Water Security Series, 2009.

54 Ibid.

55 Julie Wilk and Hans Bertil Wittgren (eds.), "Adapting Water Management to Climate Change," Swedish Water House Policy Brief, No. 7. SIWI, 2009.

56 Ibid.

57 Medellín-Azuara et al., "Water Management Adaptation with Climate Change."

58 Testimony of Dr. Peter H. Gleick, December 1st, 2010.

59 Ibid.

60 Wilk and Wittgren, "Adapting Water Management to Climate Change."

61 Matthews and Quesne, "Adapting Water Management."

62 Wilk and Wittgren, "Adapting Water Management to Climate Change."

63 Matthews and Le Quesne, "Adapting Water Management."

64 Ibid.

65 Ibid.

66 Ibid.

67 Ibid.

68 Ibid.

69 Ibid.

70 Ibid.

71 Ibid.

72 Ibid.

73 Ibid.

74 Ibid.

75 Ibid.

76 Ibid.

77 Ibid.

78 Wilk and Wittgren, "Adapting Water Management to Climate Change."

79 Ibid.

80 Ibid.

81 Ibid.

82 Ibid.

83 Ibid.

84 Ibid.

85 Ibid.

86 Ibid.

87 Australian Public Service Commission, *Tackling Wicked Problems: A Public Policy Perspective*, Australian Public Service Commission, October 25, 2007.

88 Rittel, Horst W.J. and Webber, Melvin M., "Dilemmas in a General Theory of Planning," Policy Sciences 4, 1973: 155–169.

89 Braden Kowitz, Jake Knapp, and John Zeratsky. *Sprint: How to Solve Big Problems and Test New Ideas in Just Five Days*. Simon & Schuster, 2016.

90 "Home Page," Imagine H2O, www.imagineh2o.org, accessed September 20, 2017.

91 "Policy Program," Imagine H2O, www.imagineh2o.org/policy/, accessed September 20, 2017.

92 Imagine H2O, www.imagineh2o.org/policy/, accessed September 20, 2017.

93 Western Resource Advocates, *Conservation Synergy. The Case for Integrating Water and Energy Efficiency Programs*, Western Resource Advocates, 2013.

94 Will Sarni, *Beyond the Energy–Water–Food Nexus: New Strategies for 21st Century Growth*, Dō Sustainability, 2015.

95 Heather Cooley and Kristina Donnelly, *Water-Energy Synergies: Coordinating Efficiency Programs in California*, Pacific Institute, September 2013.

96 Ibid.

97 "UK Region," Climate Bonds Initiative, https://www.climatebonds.net/region/uk, accessed September 20, 2017.

98 Sarni, *Beyond the Energy–Water–Food Nexus*.

5

CREATING ABUNDANCE – THE PATH FORWARD

How can the public sector create abundance through innovation in public policy? To some stakeholders this will seem like a crazy notion: linking innovation and abundance with public policy.

Not to us, and more importantly, other stakeholders. We started this book with a quote from Franklin Roosevelt and here, near the end, a quote by his wife Eleanor is apt: "The future belongs to those who believe in the beauty of their dreams."[1]

The authors cannot posit that they have the solution and certainly not that there is only one solution.

However, they share a strong belief that water valuation presents a powerful frame and motivator for positive action toward sustainable solutions: valuation of water services from the perspective of public infrastructure to deliver safe drinking water and provide sanitation, as well as valuation of ecosystem services related to water. Importantly, we preface our thoughts by stating such valuation is not sufficient when considering respect, protection, and fulfilment of human rights to water and sanitation.

We quote Pope Francis, where, in *Laudato Si'* he argues that "Economic valuations of water must be subordinated to frameworks of human rights."[2] Also, as Dr. Christiane Peppard wrote in her essay *Hydrology, Theology, and Laudato Si'*, "Markets are not sufficiently attentive to fundamental obligations stemming from human dignity."[3]

However, the initial provision and upkeep of infrastructure to provide and sustain water and sanitation rights does benefit from a pragmatic measure of market valuation. Similarly, the market valuation of ecosystem services is powerful enough to justify and motivate watershed protection measures, with such healthy watersheds providing the supplies of water for people. Finally, a hydro-economic analysis across the Nexus of food, water, and energy security has proven to be a transformative basis for government action and policy changes.

As previously discussed, there is a commodification of water and the human right to water. Distinguishing between water the *substance* and water *services* is quite helpful.

In the Thomas Jefferson Memorial in Washington, DC, there are inscriptions in stone regarding inalienable rights, as related to Jefferson's *Declaration of Independence*. In the context of water, one could argue that water the substance almost transcends rights. Rights exist to the living and life only exists, as we know it, with water. With that perspective, and in the context of access to safe drinking water, if you speak only of water you conflate the substance with the service.

Next, there exists a broad coalition of economists, industry, academia, and civil society that is working to develop methodologies to value nature – the Natural Capital Coalition – with the hope that such valuations will move business and policy decisions to go beyond basic pricing of land/real estate and the intuitive and aesthetic appreciation of nature, to one that allows for the cost/ benefit analysis of what natural systems provide.

The focus includes the ecosystem services that nature provides, and such services are already extensively being applied by the Nature Conservancy (TNC) and others. In some 20 'water funds' in Latin America and Africa, TNC is partnering with local governments, communities, and industry to establish transparent public/ private financing schemes that identify and protect source water areas with demonstrated benefits to downstream water quantity, quality, and flood control. Where land use changes are required, the fund also provides compensation to mainly rural farmers and communities. In effect, this approach extends the responsibility of the municipal water services provider to the ultimate upstream supply source within the watershed, and allows for the entire community and economy to play a role in its preservation.

The final example is also the most significant. The 2030 Water Resources Group (2030 WRG) is a mix of private sector, civil society, multi-lateral development banks, and foreign assistance agencies of a few European nations. 2030 WRG has been successful in 12 countries in engaging the prime ministers/presidents and finance ministers as initial sponsors to bridge the gaps between often-conflicting ministries across the Nexus.

The approach uses water as a lens, the denominator in the equation so to speak, in conducting hydro-economic analyses across the economy and compared to the government's own growth and development plans. The year 2030 is in the name of the organization as the forecast date to accomplish reform and this of course aligns with the SDG timeframe. The approach identifies gaps in water supplies needed to meet current and projected shortfalls in attaining security.

The true power is the formation of extensive, multi-stakeholder platforms to socialize and agree on data, explore and even pilot potential solutions, and ultimately let all have a voice in tradeoffs and the often-tough choices that need to be made to close gaps and grow sustainably.

All of this takes time but is designed to give government policymakers what they need to make a decision: they need to understand the facts and choices and know that their constituency does as well. They also need to have solutions proven. Most importantly, they need time and engagement for all to face realities of the choices to be made. In the end, it falls to governments to transform their policies.

2030 WRG has already seen success in Peru, with its first groundwater tariff on industry, with large-scale irrigation water conveyance system improvements in South Africa, and with widespread irrigation efficiency investments in India.

The Nexus solution framework

A framework for solutions to the energy–water–food Nexus is illustrated in Figure 5.1.[4]

Note the "soft path" and "collective action" quadrants of the framework and its relationship with the "connectivity" and "resource productivity" quadrants. While it is relatively easy to

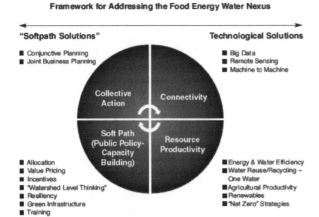

Framework for Addressing the Food Energy Water Nexus

"Softpath Solutions"   Technological Solutions

- Conjunctive Planning
- Joint Business Planning

- Big Data
- Remote Sensing
- Machine to Machine

Collective Action   Connectivity

Soft Path (Public Policy- Capacity Building)   Resource Productivity

- Allocation
- Value Pricing
- Incentives
- "Watershed Level Thinking"
- Resiliency
- Green Infrastructure
- Training

- Energy & Water Efficiency
- Water Reuse/Recycling – One Water
- Agricultural Productivity
- Renewables
- "Net Zero" Strategies

Figure 5.1 **A framework for solutions to the energy–water–food Nexus**

Source: Will Sarni, *Beyond the Energy–Water–Food Nexus: New Strategies for 21st Century Growth,* Dō Sustainability, 2015.

focus on technology solutions to address the Nexus, the soft path/ collective action strategies are essential to scale solutions and their impacts to the public and private sectors.

Stakeholder ecosystems and the golden triangle

Underpinning the soft path/collective action is the rapid adoption of business ecosystems. To best understand the role and power of business ecosystems, we recommend reading Eamonn Kelly's *Business Ecosystems Come of Age.*[5] In particular, the Introduction and the chapter on "Wicked Opportunities."

The term "ecosystems" was developed by Arthur Tansley in the 1930s to describe a localized community of living organisms interacting with each other. These organisms compete, collaborate, share, and create resources and coevolve – adapting together. In 1993, James Moore built on this concept and framed it for a business setting:[6]

> Successful businesses are those that evolve rapidly and effectively. Yet innovative businesses can't evolve in a vacuum. They must attract resources of all sorts, drawing in capital, partners, suppliers, and customers to create cooperative networks . . .

I suggest that a company be viewed not as a member of a single industry but as part of a business ecosystem that crosses a variety of industries. In a business ecosystem, companies co-evolve capabilities around a new innovation: They work cooperatively and competitively to support new products, satisfy customer needs, and eventually incorporate the next round of innovations.

According to Kelly,[7] technology companies built business ecosystems through "user communities." These companies were building technologies and platforms to connect customers and partners. However, the strategy of building ecosystems to address the energy–water–food Nexus is just emerging.

A key characteristic of the transition to business ecosystems is the blurring of boundaries between stakeholders, technologies, and roles (Figure 5.2). These business ecosystems create new opportunities and value for participating stakeholders – they are designed to: 1) make money/create value; 2) delight customers; 3) address social challenges; and 4) create, service, and deploy communities (Figure 5.3). The value in these ecosystems can be in addressing social challenges – now consider the opportunities to address public policy at the energy–water–food Nexus.

Acceleration of One of the Longest-Standing Trends in Business

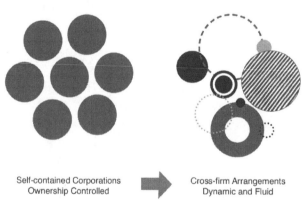

Self-contained Corporations
Ownership Controlled

Cross-firm Arrangements
Dynamic and Fluid

Figure 5.2 **Evolution of business ecosystems**

Source: Adapted from Eamonn Kelly, *Business Ecosystems Come of Age,* Deloitte University Press, 2015.

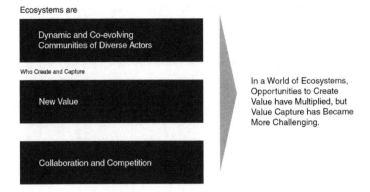

Leading to the Rise of Business Ecosystems

Ecosystems are

Dynamic and Co-evolving
Communities of Diverse Actors

Who Create and Capture

New Value

In a World of Ecosystems,
Opportunities to Create
Value have Multiplied, but
Value Capture has Became
More Challenging.

Collaboration and Competition

Figure 5.3 **Defining business ecosystems and value creation**

Source: Adapted from Eamonn Kelly, *Business Ecosystems Come of Age*, Deloitte University Press, 2015.

Eamonn Kelly defines business ecosystems as (Figure 5.3) "Dynamic and co-evolving communities of diverse actors who create and capture new value through increasingly sophisticated models of both collaboration and competition."[8]

According to Kelly, there are five ways to think about business ecosystems. They are:

- Create new ways to address fundamental human needs and desires;
- Drive new collaborations to address rising social and environmental challenges;
- Create and serve communities and harness their creativity and intelligence;
- Business ecosystems often exist on top of powerful new business platforms;
- Accelerate learning and innovation.

Consider how an energy–water–food ecosystem can be built with diverse actors to drive public policy innovation and what this might look like. A roadmap of moving from public policy silos to partnerships between the public sector, private sector, and civil society that can focus on and develop innovative solutions for economic development and incentivize policy and new business models is illustrated in Figure 5.4.

The energy–water–food ecosystem is essentially leveraging the collective knowledge and experience of businesses, government and civil society. This "golden triangle" framed by The Coca-Cola Company and forming the basis of their collective action programs is illustrated in Figure 5.5.

What does this energy–water–food ecosystem or a golden triangle look like in practice? How does this mindset and strategy create an impact at scale?

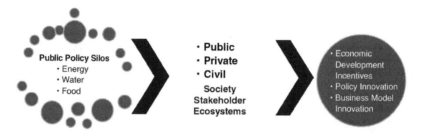

Figure 5.4 **The role of ecosystems in public policy innovation to address the energy–water–food Nexus**

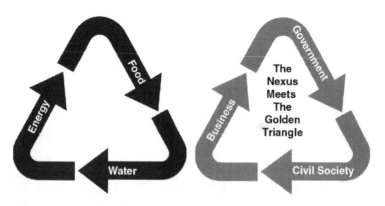

Figure 5.5 **The golden triangle to address the energy–water–food Nexus**

Source: The Coca-Cola Company, 2017.

Building stakeholder ecosystems

Building stakeholder ecosystems is not easy but it is possible. When they come to life they create value at scale and have a positive impact. One such example of building an ecosystem at scale to accelerate economic growth with associated social benefit is in Denver, Colorado.

Let's look at a current effort in Denver, where entrepreneurs have created initiatives to drive economic development, innovation, and improved quality of life. Our interview with Sean Campbell, the founder and CEO of Formativ Company, provides insights.

Sean is founder and CEO of Formativ, a real estate and economic development firm specializing in innovative commercial and mixed-use projects that focus on innovative business and community-based ecosystems.

Sean is developing the new World Trade Center Denver complex in the River North community. Sean was a co-founder and co-developer of INDUSTRY, a world-class destination for technology and digital innovation that aggregates Colorado's business community into a more productive and innovative workplace.

How do you promote an environment of cross-collaboration?

Our company builds business *ecosystems*, curated business environments that combine disciplines and foster collaboration and business development. The vernacular changed over the last few years, but when we started out in this business we were building both industry-specific and broad-based "ecosystems."

At the beginning, we focused on early-stage entrepreneurial companies, then we moved into mid-stage companies, and then more established, international companies and support systems, all located under one roof; allowing like-minded businesses a chance to share services and opportunities.

"Curated" in terms of what?

Looking at a workplace and collaborative efforts, as well as the business marketplace, to not only foster innovation, but address pain points for businesses operating within a similar industry.

For us, that's looking at the three legs to a stool: access to capital, access to markets, and attraction and retention of talent. To do this, it's about having businesses and entrepreneurs under one roof who work within a similar field. Then, establishing strong mentorship opportunities, the right educational component, which can come from private entities *or* public – but preferably from both – and finally building-in the necessarily *physical* elements that make it all come together. Our development company specializes in just that.

Our collaborative office efforts at INDUSTRY have been focused on a creative and tech-based ecosystem. There, we've got 70 different companies, and 700 people, ranging in complexity from you and I at a desk with seed capital from Mom and Dad, all the way up to a 28,000-square-foot national health lifestyle tenant, and everybody in between. Companies like Uber, Cloud Elements, Roximity, and Global Velocity.

Curating these ecosystems is looking at the *whole lifecycle* of companies and facilitating interactions of opportunities, of people, of ideas, and capital. You're aggregating best-in-breed in this programming space to help support these folks to *grow themselves* and their business.

Wouldn't it be easier to work exclusively with mature operations and technologies?

We've been heavily involved in start-ups since the get-go. We take a little different approach than your typical landlord because we're helping to curate a successful business ecosystem that *everybody* can be plugged into, and then watching companies grow within our buildings, or grow out of them. If you work with mature operations, their ecosystem is already established and there tends to be less collaboration.

For example, with the World Trade Center we've been assessing what the great industries are that we have in the state: energy, clean tech, bio, healthcare, and aerospace. And then there's ones that are *starting* to emerge: cyber technology, agricultural innovation, water technology and innovation, the nexus of ag/water/energy and food. So, part of what we've been doing on the

World Trade Center is starting to curate some of those *opportunities* representing the next phase of Denver's economy and recognizing that there is a lot of overlap between these industries, so what better than to provide an office building of the future for them to call home so to foster more innovation, collaboration, business development, and in turn, economic growth.

Can you create a collaborative workspace anywhere? How dependent is it on the larger, municipal or regional environment?

For the most part, yes, because it's more than just a space to have a meet-up. When we won and started tackling the World Trade Center project, I said clearly that we need to create a physical space for the entity and, most importantly, define what the ingredients are going to go into this place; we call this the ecosystem. It's the ecosystem that "solves the problem" for the area, its tenants, etc. that creates a community that could be sustained in a major city or a smaller town, perhaps just with different features and functionality.

For WTC Denver, we decided that if the city, and broader Front Range region, is going to grow up and become more prominent on the global stage, we need to evaluate what are we doing well, what *aren't* we doing, and where are the gaps. Doing this gap analysis led us to the ways we can attract some of the talent, capital, market opportunity to our back yard to strengthen the local entrepreneurial ecosystem.

Denver has done a good job supporting these collaborative ecosystems. It's been a *collective* mash up between the city, developers, businesses, and entrepreneurs, driven by the innovation culture in our city.

What other kinds of local intellect does the immediate area offer to support the entrepreneurial spirit?

We've got a very collaborative DNA in the state, unlike anywhere else I've worked, whether it's been in New York, or DC, or on the (West) Coast. I think people are willing to roll up their sleeves for a good idea even if it's not their own, and go and try to get it done. That's been from the governor's office, the mayor's office, the chamber, as well as C-suites around town. I think that's a key ingredient that you can't replicate everywhere and something you're not going to see in the major markets anytime soon.

We've got 30-plus national research labs in this state. More than inside the Beltway. NREL and UCAR, and NCAR, and NASA, and NOAA. They're all thought of as Beltway organizations. But UCAR and NCAR have 1,400 people, and *1,375 are in Colorado.* They have 20 in DC, and they have five on a mountain in Hawaii, but these guys doing the cutting-edge work are here in Colorado. They're better known globally than they are domestically just because of the efforts they're making in climate change and in renewable energies. What we've been trying to do here is connect the dots. How we cross-pollinate different industries on the private side can help places like the UAE in Dubai to help guide how *their* next generation of growth is founded.

It's this culture in Denver that has allowed us to think the way we have about the DNA of the World Trade Center Denver project. It's partnering with these labs, public and private sectors, entrepreneurs, and major global businesses within a building of the future. For example, it takes a typical US citizen two or three weeks to get on the campus at NREL. So, what we've pitched with these labs is saying let's get some of the technology, some of that expertise from behind the curtain and out here into the public. Let's set up an expo center, like what you and I would think exists at MIT or Stanford's tech transfer office. So, you can say, "Hey, as an organization, I may not always be able to depend on financing from Washington. I need to become more self-sufficient as an organization, and I want to start partnering with countries, private industries, and public municipalities." So, part of what we're doing is helping organizations like NREL and UCAR/NCAR think differently about how they're partnering and collaborating with others, and giving them a platform to do that in their backyard, in Colorado.

I think that the chamber, and the city fathers over the years have done a really great job getting us from 80 percent relying on energy to 20 percent and having – as you said, a hugely diversified economy across about 10 different major industries, and then helping support these next stage ones like the food, and water, and the ag, and cyber securities that are already knocking on the door with the labs, and some of the higher ed things. We could own water, and some of the ag innovation stuff worldwide right here in our backyard, and if Dubai wants to come over and beta test something, or Monsanto's got something in the works that they want to prop up with CSU, we've got the right DNA to get that done.

What are the obstacles in the intersection of these organizations you are curating under one roof?

Part of what's at the core of the World Trade Center Denver organization and our team, is to provide a building, an eco-system, that eliminates as many obstacles as possible. We really want to help these companies think beyond their own business silo; start thinking more *collectively* to realize that thinking, technology, and capital can be shared, and it's this cross-pollination of innovation that ends up actually moving the needle.

Is public policy taking a back seat to international and corporate engagement at this point?

If you're in any business, and you're not necessarily scaling it, you're waiting for a check out of Washington, or some foundation, that's not a very sustainable or scalable kind of model. And so, I think a lot of the labs are thinking that even though they're NGOs, or government agencies, and they aren't in the business of "being in business," they're self-described *bad* marketers, or branders of what they do. But if they don't start thinking about how they can be a little more sustainable, even if it means they get the same check out of DC, or appropriations, great. But there's a ton of business that sits on the sidelines because of the way the "traditional" way they've done things is not particularly innovative when they're thinking about growing their own organization. They might be the most innovative on the planet at launching a weather satellite, but that doesn't mean that makes it to a business model, which they're all living under whether they like it or not.

We're pushing them to think that way, because we just think that makes good business sense, and it's high reward with very little risk. These are existing, proven technologies, whether they were created for DOE, or DOD, or private industry, and some of them are in the public domain, or can be licensed with the lab in partnership. So, we're thinking that it just makes good sense no matter who's in office in DC, or whatever foundation check you're attached to, to be looking for a sustainable new business model where you're not asking for a handout every year.

You said there were lots of "little" risks?

What I mean by that is that the labs themselves are huge organizations. They've got a lot of different things going on, but what they also have is a lot of incredibly smart scientists that would love to engage with a big multinational. Think GE, or Arrow, or something like that. Or Lockheed, where they're working together on a technology that they're developed, or vice versa, and there's a cost, or there's a fee-based service that they have.

There's several different models within the lab, where they can partner without a lot of risk. They're still going to have their 1,375 folks working there. They likely have some unused bandwidth, and they have technologies that they could license out, with approval, for very little risk. These have already been created. They can be weather forecasting tools, or renewables, or micro grids, or smart houses, or efficient technologies that they're working on for the home, or for commercial. In terms of risk, what I mean is that they could engage in a pretty serious business development opportunity in the short term without spending a bunch of political, real, or otherwise capital on setting that up.

Tell us about the successes to date, where you see you're getting traction combining disparate disciplines for a common outcome.

There's been some successes. As an example, UCAR, NCAR is partnered with the country of Taiwan, and they're going to launch six satellites as a team, so those organizations are laying off costs, Taiwan gets a benefit as a country outside the US. And those are launching as we speak, this year. Then there's smaller wins. The sustainable building group over at NREL is working with developers and builders on micro apartments and efficient urban housing. So, as this "affordable" housing pain point rises in the marketplace, there are some modular homes that they're looking at, and some of them are done with big national corporations like Lennar Homes, or they're done on a smaller subset, where they're partnering with Toshiba, or Samsung, or others in terms of just how the appliances inside the building work, whether it's laundry, or dishwasher.

On our organization side you can look at 10.10.10, which is Tom Higley's initiative to address 10 wicked problems in health or in cities, using 10 perspectives, from successful CEOs looking for their next thing, and do it in 10 days. And they're mashing up these ideas and opportunities here in Denver as well as in other cities around the country. They've launched *several* companies. On average, over the last three years I think they're about 40 or 50 percent of those CEOs and the resources that they gather up in those conferences are starting to match up and get funding. So, that's a really interesting new model. You're looking at wicked subsets of *big* problems and the market opportunities and matching up with proven CEOs, and capital to take the next step, to be that disruptor on whatever that might be.

How are you envisioning the Nexus proposition, the water–energy–food intersection, from a regional context?

What's happening here now is that we all see these crazy figures about population growth, not just in our little city here in Denver, but this migration to these pretty dense and populated areas everywhere. What does that look like in terms of urban food, and food solutions, and food security? What does that look like for water, and some of these crazy desalination projects?

When you look at what are the challenges, and opportunities within *water*, what are possibilities in ag innovations, and much of it points to *urban food* solutions and other things as these populations grow. To build that, we've got a lot of incredible "natural" resources in terms of educational power, and know-how, and knowledge here in the state. CSU is building a huge ag innovation program along with Denver and the state, with Denver Water, at the National Western Complex. They're starting a water and ag innovation center alongside an equine rehabilitation and innovation center.

In our region *energy* is going to be a lot bigger focus here than it might be somewhere else. And so, there's a lot of opportunities whether it's clean tech, or renewables, or otherwise around that, and I think when you leverage state and city efforts alongside with labs and really smart private sector folks, you start to attract talent and capital, and then you're off to the races. Then you have the ability to start to fund early-stage companies, get them out them, beta test them, slingshot them, quickly understand pain points or where you need to pivot, and get them to scale or at least starting to scale. And I think that Denver and the region has done a very good job at that.

How urgent is the water–food–energy Nexus on the horizon?

It's only going to grow, and it's not like degrees, if you look on some dashboard at the analytics of degrees of who's "winning the race." It's like, "How screwed are you on that list? Are you orange, are you red, or are you purple?" If we don't start thinking of it as that Nexus, and having pretty frank discussions, across industries, private, public, higher education, or otherwise, if you don't break down some of the silos so that you're tackling these things together, then you will be operating in the purple before you know it. But we have an opportunity here to show people how that collaboration, how that team work can work, and then we can export that around the globe, and own it *as a region.*

For example, we were over in Dubai visiting with their leadership, looking some of their innovation centers. Here's a country built on a place that's 120 degrees in the shade, eight months out of the year. They've got no water. They desalinate every bit of their water, and they grow no food. And our take was, "I understand you're looking for what's next after your mineral reserves are gone, but maybe agriculture is not the highest and best use of that desert."

Implementing Nexus solutions at scale

Another view of the energy–water–food Nexus challenges and opportunities from a public sector and academic lens is from Dr. Rabi Mohtar, TEES Research Professor at Texas AM University, College Station, Texas.

Dr. Rabi Mohtar, TEES Research Professor, Department of Biological and Agricultural Engineering and Zachry Department of Civil Engineering, Texas A&M University, leads the Water Energy Food Nexus Initiative and the Water Energy Food Research Group. Mohtar was founding director of Qatar Environment and Energy Research Institute (QEERI) a member of Qatar Foundation, Research and Development and the Founding Director, Strategic Projects, Qatar Foundation Research and Development. He was also the inaugural Director of Purdue University's Global Engineering Programs in West Lafayette, Indiana.

Mohtar's primary research priority is the development of a framework to quantify the interlinkages of the energy–water–food Nexus as constrained by climate change and social, political, and technological pressures.

Mohtar served the World Economic Forum Global Agenda Council on Water Security from 2009–2011, and serves its Climate Change Agenda Council since 2011. He is on the Board of Governors of the World Water, and the Advisory Board of the UNFCC Momentum of Change Initiative, among many other global leadership roles. Dr. Mohtar has published over 300 publications, including peer-reviewed articles, refereed conference proceedings, book chapters, and books. Among his numerous international research honors are the Kishida International award for contributions to agricultural research, American Society of Agricultural and Biological Engineers (ASABE) and the Ven Te Chow Memorial Lecture Award of the International Water Resources Association (IWRA).

Your work on the topic of public policy in support of the energy–water–food Nexus came to light officially with the World Economic Forum Global Agenda Council in 2011. How long had this been in the making?

I started thinking about these interactions back in 2000, while I was teaching. I began to see this as a series of linkages (between water, energy, and food) but the first public activity occurred in 2009, when we started the discussion about water security. Earlier, I was more into research and teaching and was bringing these interlinkages to the classroom while feeling the need to push the concept further.

What kind of challenges and obstacles have you seen when you talk to people about this?

I remember when we first started to speak about the Nexus back in the early days, the general challenge we faced was that, conceptually, it makes sense that the relationship between, water, energy, food exists. Okay, so what? What do I do with that knowledge? How do I show some applications and real-life examples? I realized then that we needed quantification and analytics to support the conceptual framework.

That's when I took a step back and started developing the analytics. The question of "so what?" began making sense once we started the analytics and case studies: we found some complete, real-life examples. The challenge that still exists is that the axis is somehow confused: there is a lack of appreciation and understanding, but also a fear that "Nexus is coming and going to take over the water, energy and food disciplines". So, I think that the challenge we face is how to ensure that the stakeholders see *the added value* that Nexus thinking carries so that they don't feel threatened by a new inter-disciplinary platform.

The Nexus does not replace any disciplinary activity; it *leverages and synergizes* what's already happening in integrated water resources management regarding *energy efficiency and water productivity*. Those remain the very essential elements upon which the Nexus builds. Today, the challenge to have success stories where we are able to demonstrate how much money and resources were saved: "this is how much primary resources were saved in using the Nexus approach". Today, a large-scale, successful Nexus implementation is necessary to establish the case that Nexus is the way forward.

If analytics are the next step, how long and how involved is the process to start quantifying this issue?

We are working on this: you cannot excessively generalize. The principles and the reason are general, and you develop assumptions to model the system using a structured systems representation. *But, in the Nexus, everything is about local resources* and building a model depends on the scale, everything is dependent upon where the questions are coming from: there are many dimensions, and it is hard to generalize the analytics.

We have been working on *standardizing* the way in which we approach the analytics and the data: local data will actually shape the analytics. We have several schematics and regional applications who's only similarity is the process used to develop the analytics, which have proven to be very much a unique experience each time that we move from one activity to another. Everything is embedded in local specificity, which makes it difficult to generalize.

So, one question is: down the road, do we want a system of systems model that develops the general analytics for *all* schematic and scale issues? Perhaps, but that is going to take years to build and short of having this comprehensive, multi-scale, multi-themed analytic, we need to develop a protocol.

The question becomes: "How do you collect the relevant data at the scale that is universal?"

So, with an issue so dependent on locality, how do you build larger scale strategy?

The *local* is not only governed by the geophysical, but also by governments and the governance structure created by them for these resources. It's governed by *who* is asking the questions: the manager of that watershed basin? The farmer? The practitioner? A concerned citizen? Each of these has different questions and all of these questions drive different prophecies in the analytics. We have had success in promoting the principles: the guidelines coupled with successful examples.

Are there any similarities from one watershed or one nationality to the next as far as how you get public policy wrapped around the idea of energy, food, and water all being part of the same issue? How do we get the legislative process on board with that?

The policymakers want to do the right thing: they need to see how much more they could save, both financially but also in resources, through *policy-coherent, science-informed decision-making.* Until we have a large-scale, successful implementation of the Nexus and are able to advises policymakers to adopt a policy, we must rely on a great deal on basic awareness that what we are saying does makes sense. The analytics are just not there, yet, to build a large-scale case.

On what kind of scale are you seeing success?

We do have several successful examples at the watershed scale, at the industry scale, and potentially at the national scale with implementation of the SDGs. But all of these are preliminary calculations pending additional data and evaluation. It takes time to build confidence in the analytics and then to follow what the analytics is saying.

For instance, we've been doing several national plans. If you take country "x" and do the analytics and the tradeoffs, our calculations and modeling indicate that it saves the national government *cash and resources* to do a policy coherence in the Nexus, rather than to maintaining the "silos" (discrete) decision process. We have the analytics to support our recommendation, but it takes *years* for the government to step back and say, "we are working on restructuring the decision-making process to allow for *communication across sectors.*" That structure doesn't yet exist.

How successful have government entities been in listening to and adopting fresh thinking based on scientific strategy?

It's not consistent at all. I see pockets of excellence in several; yet there are agencies at the local level simply not much on board: there's no consistency at all. Agencies that see the value are pushing, promoting coherence between the water, energy, food sectors; and I see some uncertainty over the last several months. Eventually we will realize the need for interagency interaction to allow better coherence and decision making, but that hasn't happened yet. Recent years seem to have brought more opportunity for interagency dialogues.

Are there pilot projects that are providing feedback?

We have several pilot projects: one that's taking most of my current time is the San Antonio pilot project, in which we've been working on several dimensions of the Nexus. The idea is to understand *all* of the interactions that exist, including the biophysical level, the policy level, the data modeling, the tradeoffs, and the agency-stakeholder interactions. We're also trying to look at technologies. So, we have all these dimensions that are important in the Nexus dialogue and are trying to understand them at the local, manageable scale before we scale up to state and national levels.

Those are some disparate disciplines you are engaging.

This is a university-wide effort; we've a few dozen faculty and grad students working on it: it's not a small initiative. And there are several international projects addressing the SDGs, including projects in Turkey, the Mekong River basin, and the Middle East. We've got several of these schematic and regional projects overseas; but our biggest case study is San Antonio, because it has all of the dimensions.

Is it too early to draw any conclusions? What are you finding out about this?

Way too early: the challenge is very complex and this is our first year. We're moving in parallel so that we have time to understand the stakeholders, who call the shots for water/energy/food. We are trying to understand the supply chains and the decision-making processes, but we're also trying to build the models and tools, the analytics, for this interaction. We're trying to look at low-hanging fruit: as food technologies impacting water and energy, and food that will reduce the footprint of all three. It's a complex mosaic of Nexus projects.

Have there been any instances of innovation with regard to policy coherence that you can point to that you are learning?

That's going to be the biggest issue in San Antonio, and other locations: the first step is to build trust. One of the first issues actually is emerging are questions like: "Why are you doing this?" "What's in it for me?" and "How do I make sure that I can open my books across sectors?" There are many challenges in developing the policy coherence: a lot of skeptics, a lot of business-as-usual thinking. The analytics, science, and technology align, but trying to persuade policymakers and decision-makers in industry that the intent is building trust will be a challenge. The incentive structure is not there for the disciplines to cooperate.

Who do you think is going to take the lead in this? Which sector do you think it will come from? Public, private, civic?

Eventually, probably all of the above, but I'm hoping that informed citizens will put some pressure on public policymakers. I don't know if the public is actually aware yet of the

Nexus and its potential to improve the security of our primary resources. It's still too early because the public doesn't yet know what the Nexus is. For this reason, we've started actually interacting with civil society in the San Antonio region to elevate awareness, but we have a long distance to go.

A big part of our effort is engaging our stakeholders: we have several meetings planned with the San Antonio stakeholders, including the public and private sectors and the decision-makers in public policy.

Do you think it will be more influenced at the outset by economics or by policy?

We haven't yet looked at governance models and what needs to happen. What is clear is that there needs to be better policy coherence. If you look at a nexus solution, it does not belong to a single sector: who does own it? How is it going to be financed? How is it going to be managed? At the moment, we don't have the governance structure that allows managing these interdisciplinary solutions. We need to be thinking down the road, "How do you build the structure to implement solutions that sit at the borders between water, energy, and food?"

How has your organization's credibility influenced the rate of adoption?

The advantage we have, at the end of the day, is that we're not a think tank or a public policy institute. We're an institution for research and higher education that carries out research and development. We are expected to generate more knowledge, in terms of the modeling, the tools, the technologies that will reduce the dependencies that water and energy and food have on one another. With improved knowledge, we will work with entities at the other end of the science – decision-making spectrum, who will say: "Now that we know better, how do we improve our decision-making processes?"

The goal of this whole exercise is a better understanding of the interlinkages, a better understanding of what technology, which tools work best. But when it comes to changing public policy, it is going to take further effort. We intend to publish and disseminate knowledge to the public about alternative management approaches for water, energy, food in San Antonio. I believe that this will be a success story to be shared: the first step in influencing decision-making.

So, you are looking at a two-year timeframe for the San Antonio effort?

Yes, our target is two years to show some innovative solutions for Texas resource management. Our benchmark is, "Do we have better ways that can better inform policymakers?" The second challenge then becomes: once we have those ways, how do we communicate them? How do we encourage better decisions based on the knowledge we gained?

What are you finding encouraging at this point?

People get the concept. The implementation challenges: financing and policy coherence represent a major, big deal. But, as a scientist, if I can communicate a solution that makes sense on paper, how do transform into implementation? Who's going to finance it? How do you build the policy-coherence structure? That probably is one of those issues that we will be battling for a long time after we have some innovative solutions. Moving from solution to implementation will be a challenge.

Another couple of views of how the golden triangle ecosystem can create value and innovation at scale are from the FEMSA Foundation and the World Bank. First an interview with Mariano Montero Zubillaga, director of Fundación FEMSA.

Let's start with the work that you've done on the Nexus of water, energy, and food. What are some of the things that have been happening? What are some of the challenges? What's some of the progress that you've made?

FEMSA Foundation (FF) was established in 2008 and it was decided to channel most of its resources into water conservation. Being FEMSA, basically a beverage company and the largest Coca-Cola independent bottler, water availability has always been a critical resource for the sustainability of our business. The bottling operation was heavily committed to have the most water efficient processes "fenced-in," that is to say that the water used in the bottling process was efficiently used and any discharge to the sewer system was adequately treated. But this did not either help return to nature the water included in the products, nor guarantee the long-term availability of water for the operation.

These objectives implied protecting the water source. This task cannot be achieved by one individual company, and the beneficiary is the community served by the watershed.

FF together with the Inter-American Development Bank (IDB), the Nature Conservancy (TNC) and the Global Environmental Facility (GEF), promoted the creation of a civil society organization, Water Funds (WF), bringing together private companies, academia, and government institutions, to promote and finance conservation projects through green infrastructure in the upper watersheds.

To date, the partnership has launched 19 WF throughout Latin America, mobilizing close to $120 million in the last five years. WFs also aim at participating and influencing the governance structure for water, thus helping achieve water security for the communities where we operate.

The other area where FF participates is bringing clean water and sanitation to communities that do not have access to this resource. Through the first phase of our program "Lazos de Agua" and partnering with the Coca-Cola Foundation and Millennium Water Alliance, we mobilized internal and external resources for an amount of $11 million to bring water and sanitation to 110,000 people in five countries in Latin America. We are now preparing the second phase of this program, this time with a stronger partnership including One Drop (Cirque de Solei Foundation), the IDB and Coca-Cola, bringing innovation to the field in the form of social arts as a means to change behaviors related to water conservation and hygiene habits.

You talked about water funds. How are those structured?

I am convinced that we need different solutions to the traditional way we have approached many problems in our society, including water. We need a more active civil society and structures in which they can participate. In particular, I think the business sector has a lot to offer to our traditional practices, in which we leave all the burden to governments.

WFs, as I mentioned, provide a space for the private business sector to participate in water-related issues. Through the partnership FF has with the IDB, TNC, and the GEF, we identify cities suffering from water stress conditions which could benefit from watershed conservation through green infrastructure. TNC recommends specific conservation projects, then we then identify business people with special interest in water conservation and propose the formation of a WF. One of them is invited to chair the WF. Also, the partnership invests seed money to finance pilot projects and motivate the business community to become part of the fund and donate resources to continue investing in green infrastructure. In our experience, local and regional governments welcome this participation and open spaces for the WF to become an active participant in the water ecosystem.

How do you get so many different people into the same room?

In a recent paper, the OECD identified governance as one of the most relevant opportunities for effective and efficient water resources management. WFs seek to identify key players in the water management system and propose an open dialog to identify long-range objectives and plans to achieve water security in their particular regions. It is not easy, as many important players have different and sometimes conflicting agendas. We try to work as a team.

IDB has important participation as a source of financial resources for water-related projects, so their invitation to government institutions is very helpful. The business people forming part of the WF usually wield important influence in their region, so their invitation to participate in these dialogs is highly valued. Local governments are, of course, interested in providing adequate supply of water to their cities, so they welcome the opportunity to be part of this initiative.

All these actors and participants seek the same end result: water security. We start by convincing some of them to start talking about the future of availability for their regions. Then you get more people involved. You bring information, projections, the best possible science applied to diagnose the watershed health and sustainability. The idea is to form a critical mass that will push the envelope to bring the water security issue to a top position on the regional agenda.

It sounds like there is a fairly high awareness that water resources are under stress. Is that accurate to say?

There is enough evidence that water is one of the most critical risks in many Latin American cities: 16 of the 20 largest cities in the region experience water stress. Three of the six most problematic cities in the world with serious water security problems – Mexico City, Lima, and Rio de Janeiro – are in our sub-continent.

FF together with IDB have sponsored the Tecnologico de Monterrey, one of the most prestigious private universities in Mexico, to form the Water Center for Latin America and the Caribbean. Recently we released a publication titled *Water and Cities in Latin America,* where the water-related challenges for sustainable development are clearly identified.

What can you tell me about collective action in your arena? What is happening there?

Collective action is at the root of the WF's strategy. To have any influence in water governance, first you need to identify the main actors that participate in this ecosystem and bring them to the table, where we can discuss long-range objectives and establish a common agenda. The next challenge is to create governance mechanisms to monitor the activities and progress of the different stakeholders. These mechanisms vary from region to region because we have to be able to adapt our strategy to different local and regional particularities.

There is a need to open new governance alternatives for the civil society and the business community to participate. Particularly I am convinced that the business sector offers long-range planning capabilities as well as efficient and effective use of resources. Some WFs have been able to convince local authorities to establish a percentage of water tariffs to go into conservation projects which are defined and supervised by the WFs.

Our model is, in this country (the US) we have these huge silos, especially in the government. The Department of Energy doesn't talk to Agriculture and that sort of thing. Are you seeing the same thing in Mexico?

I think it's the same thing. Again, I have been talking with the agro sectors and they don't have water-saving activities in their agenda, but they have very good ideas. So when I question them and ask "What can we do to save water?" they say, "Well that's not on my agenda, but we can identify areas where we could implement modern irrigation systems that could save water and at the same time increase crop productivity."

Just to give you an example of the opportunities we have by breaking those silos, in the city of Monterrey we had a huge hurricane in 2010 which destroyed an important part of freeways at both sides of a riverbed that was completely flooded. The reconstruction of this infrastructure cost the city close to $1 billion. With a fraction of this money we could have prevented this destruction by investing in the upper shed with a combination of green and grey infrastructure. These are communication opportunities that need to be opened.

What about within the energy industry? Are you seeing the same thing? Are they thinking about ways of conserving water?

There is a growing interest as well as investments in new renewable sources of energy. Also it is important to consider that Mexico is going through an important energy reform that will bring new players, where before, only government could participate. In the years to come I am sure this Nexus between energy and water will be addressed.

Is a common valuation on water an issue for you at this point? Or are you dealing more with higher-level concepts and practices that aren't really tied to finite metrics?

One of the things that we're trying to do is to develop new tools to make better business cases for investments in water and other sustainability projects. Water savings and water conservation have to prove to be profitable investment decisions for cities and societies. But often times, you don't have the tools to bring objectivity to calculate a return on investment.

We have been working with NYU, New York University, and ANTEA, a US consulting company, to develop a tool we call *Monetizing*. This is basically a methodology to understand the value of sustainability decisions and translate that value in dollar terms. With this, we hope to help companies make better decisions in sustainability.

Who in an organization do you approach with this? If it's government, it seems like everybody is trying to get to the foreign minister rather than just the minister of agriculture.

This is very relevant. Water is a local problem, so it has to be dealt with locally. There are of course federal agencies that are at the center of public policies and regulations, but we think that it is the local community with the local government that needs to address water security. Many of the factors affecting water security need to be addressed and solved locally. Federal agencies have to acknowledge local problems and with a broader view to facilitate the solutions, especially when they have impact in other neighboring regions.

So it sounds like there will be different people, depending on what region you're going into. Is that correct?

Yes. Because, for instance, the city of Monterrey is an industrial city. So the industry has a lot of weight and WF require an important participation from the industrial community. But in the state of Guanajuato where we are in the process of launching a WF, the main activity is agriculture. The strategy there will be to leverage the value chain of companies such as Heineken that get their agro products from the region, to influence local producers to adopt modern irrigation systems. In Mexico City, the situation is very different. The problems there are of a different magnitude and the participation of the WF will mainly be through the Rockefeller's Foundation initiative, "100 Resilient Cities."

It must take a lot of time to get into a local culture and find out what to stimulate and figure out what the local agendas are, who's in charge of it, where the momentum is going and who's making decisions. It sounds like this is an issue that occurs watershed by watershed.

That's exactly right and it's a critical decision, deciding who is going to be the champion at each watershed. We have to be able to identify somebody who has a stake in water, who uses water as an important resource, who has good connections and are well-respected, well-recognized. That way, we will be able to bring the right people to the table and develop a common agenda. It's not always easy.

Also, the way society interacts and the roles played by each sector in a specific city or even at the country level varies significantly. In some regions, governments have a leading role, with little space for other participants. In other regions, the civil society is more active and has more influence. It varies. Therefore, you have to be aware of the way society functions in each of the countries where we are active with our partnership.

Are there any other thoughts you have about the Nexus and the challenges that are in front of you that you would explain to a newcomer? What are your issues? What are you keeping your eyes on? What are you looking for?

Several things. One, of course, is to consolidate our efforts into bringing the civil society and especially the business community into the water governance system. As I mentioned before, the private sector brings continuity and accountability to the actions necessary to achieve the desired state of water security.

We mentioned the need to break the silos on which many of the current government agencies operate. There is a clear need for coordinated collective action.

One thing that we did not mention is how technology will impact the sector. When, for instance, we talk about the future of *mobility* in the cities, there are many scenarios but most coincide on the main characteristics the future of transportation will offer. In terms of water, there is, at least to the best of my knowledge, no common agenda of coincidence on how the future of water supply will take place. Will it be desalination of seawater which will become feasible as energy becomes cheaper and technology evolves? Will it be off-the-grid solutions where households will have their own supply of water and energy? These are questions we need to work on more closely.

Other issues we are trying to understand is how to make society more conscious of the need to conserve this vital resource. This has to do with water tariffs, saving water as we have learned with electricity, the need to reserve water for nature, and several other issues.

Do you see the products of these collaborations being a permanent ongoing dialogue or is it something that is going to have a beginning, middle, and end to it? You're talking about alignments between stakeholders from different areas of the economy and of the social fabric and you're getting around a table to talk about the issues and figure out some possible solutions to the idea of water availability and stewardship. Do you see this as a starting of a permanent dialogue going on? Are there going to be organizations set up in perpetuity to do this? Or is this a water council thing where you may have some sort of annual convergence happening, over a week or two?

Basically, what we are talking about is a new way to face the great challenges we as a society have. In the last century I think society commissioned governments to solve problems and bring services to communities. We have mixed results at best, especially in our region. We need different structures and organizations to tackle these challenges. Government, organized society, and academia need to get more involved and work together. This is the only way we will be able to advance and create a better future for society. This will be the new paradigm to follow. It is starting now and will continue for the years to come.

Our interview with Diego J. Rodriguez, Senior Water Resources Management Specialist at the World Bank, highlights similar issues and opportunities.

Tell us a little bit about the strategy for addressing the Nexus between water and energy. What went into approaching three so massive complexities?

This exercise started as a spin-off of the Bonn Conference (The Bonn 2011 Conference: Water, Energy and Food Security Nexus – Solutions for the Green Economy, a high-level, invitation-only conference organized by the German Federal Government in collaboration with the World Economic Forum [WEF], the World Wildlife Fund [WWF], and the International Food Policy Research Institute [IFPRI].)

We were members of the Steering Committee (SC) at the invitation of the German government. The idea was that the steering committee helped organized the Conference itself and also looked *beyond* the conference. It was the idea of this new concept on the Nexus of water, energy, and food. During the period of more than a year the SC met frequently to discuss the expected outcome of the conference. Initially it seemed as we were focusing very much at the Nexus from the *water* perspective. We are constantly looking through the water lens into how the other sectors should manage, or should use *their* resources.

We kept insisting that the Nexus had to be something different than the traditional approaches that we followed on water resources management, and that we needed to look at an *entry point* for that. In terms of water use and water consumption, you have big users in energy and big users in agriculture.

Of course, agriculture is the most complex and the sector that uses the most water. The energy sector is also a big user because water is not only used for hydropower generation, but also for cooling processes in coal, solar, and nuclear. Coal mining also requires vast amounts of water. What was needed was, really, an approach in which you can bring some practical tools to influence the large users of water.

There was ample discussions in the SC on whether these water, and energy, and food issues could be tackled *all at once in a fully integrated manner,* because we were trying to come with practical planning tools that could help not only in the planning process, but also in investment design, investment operation, and infrastructure investments. When we finished that exercise as part of the Bonn Conference, and returned to Washington, we started designing, or formulating, a World Bank initiative.

The conclusion was that it's quite a complex set of issues that each one of these main water using sectors have. It is very difficult to tackle the water problems all at once. We agreed that when we looked at some of the water problems in those spaces, we would obviously start with water balances and try to understand synergies and tradeoffs across competing sectors, and how water is allocated. Those are some of the traditional ways that we look at water resources management.

But in addition to that, we decided we would try to embed ourselves, as water experts, into the complexities of the planning and investment design framework of other sectors, to learn in much more detail the complexities of their planning and investment frameworks. The water expertise can provide a better understanding on how water is allocated, and understand the competition for that resource. Only then could we influence how the other two sectors worked.

Sounds complicated, but linear. How did the strategy play out?

At that point there was quite a bit of resistance in the energy sector, globally. This issue was gaining a lot of prominence, among the very big energy producers, but they are, basically, private sector energy producers. We thought that there would be much more appetite to get into this dialogue studying agriculture. But agriculture is very complex; socially it's very difficult, politically, as well. It's something that, from the water side, we understand much better, but the constraints are that there are more issues on the politics and social aspects in the agriculture sector.

So we started by engaging with the energy sector because our approach was, if we bring more accuracy and more understanding of the competition for water resources, and a much better understanding on the hydrological aspects in a basin, understanding much more on how water is used by the different energy technologies, we can actually help the energy sector understand that all the investments that you have in energy can *be compromised* (when water resources become stressed). There are resource constraints down the line in the near future, that cause you to either stop or slow down energy production, and you try to avoid that.

When you decided to avoid the issues with agriculture – that must have been kind of a major step for you guys at that point – to bow out of that.

It was not really to avoid them. In the first phase of the analysis that we do, we always look at the total water balance in a basin or in a country. In a very traditional first analysis of water resources management, we look at agriculture as well. We go into basins at the national scale and we understand the supply side, the hydrological assessment, on what is stream flow and rain, groundwater and evapotranspiration in a basin. That allows us to estimate how much water there is on the *supply* side.

We also look at the *demand* side, at how that water is being used. By "use" we mean its obstruction. There's a return flow to the basin, and there is *consumption,* where the water is lost to the system. We estimate the balance between supply and demand that is going on today and in that particular basin and also the projections for the future. How much is being used by each sector at a particular point in time? We really look at water use by *all* of the different sectors on the demand side balanced with the supply side. Including agriculture.

It was just that the main client, or the main entry point should *not* be agriculture at this point because of its complexities. It's not that it is ignored from the analysis, it's that in order to be able to develop practical tools we decided to work with the energy sector as our primary entry point.

At the outset, what were the biggest challenges that were facing you when you decided to focus on the energy business and go places other people had not gone before as far as coordinating the water needs?

The biggest challenge is what I keep on saying at these conferences, that we, in the water sector, work on the *management* of water. As a water expert you try to come up with management schemes, but you're not a *user* of water. It's the economic sectors that use water. Agriculture, energy, these are very powerful, proactive and growth-oriented sectors.

Most economic sectors like these, a few years back, worked under the assumption that whatever water they need, they will get. It would be available for them, there would be no constraints, because of how much they continue to grow, and the development that represents. And that is a very tough nut to crack.

So we turned the messaging around with energy so it was no longer about a "policing-type" of action, that "you should not be using more water." We were mostly saying, "If you understand the competition using resources in our sectors, in a particular basin, and get the details on how much water you are using or how much water you are consuming, *the development of planning tools that properly incorporate the water challenges can help you make better decisions* and avoid having a potential problem of stranded assets." Interruptions in process for a few days, or reducing the amount of energy that you produce, will cost you millions of dollars. There are plenty of examples already around the world where that happened.

Also, from us actually going into the energy sphere, into understanding all of *their* own planning tools, we found their planning units or finalities are different than for water, and you, basically, have to learn and adapt *your* understanding of water to *their* realities. That took us five years.

Were the energy companies aware of the fact of the brown-out threat from reduced water access? You said there were many examples already. Did they just not think it was going to apply to them? What was the awareness at the early stage?

I think it was quite limited in those early days. You can pick some examples in different regions of the world in which some power plants have to diminish production. There was much more awareness, for example, in the US. In the US you have a network of energy labs that for 15 years now have been addressing this issue of water and energy nexus, so they had quite good data examples in the US where energy companies were facing some water-related constraints already. But this was not very well known in the rest of the world.

Do you have any performance metrics for results – even early ones at this point? How are you measuring the results?

Because of the complexity of the issue, the energy sector, even the energy sector in the Bank, made much more reference to the *linkages* between water and energy (rather than metrics). When countries are starting to do a national planning exercise in energy, they can tap into our methodologies and our narratives to assess those planning frameworks (and then data will be available).

It was mainly an issue of, first on the technical side, to be able to devise a methodology in which we could incorporate the complexities of water resources and the complexities on water using energy in a way that was built from energy platforms themselves, from *their* models and *their* instruments – and we did that.

The other point is we can go to any country and based on the tools that they are currently using for planning our investment design, we now have a methodology that anything can be adopted to include the intricacies and the inter-linkages between water and energy. That was more of the technical goal that we had, where previously we were more on the advocacy side, to ensure that all of these big energy players knew us, and they get more acquainted with our initiatives and that we could be more of an influencing-slash-advocacy seeker for them. That happened because, in the last five years, we've been invited to be part of a lot of those dialogues, within the energy sector.

We are now, for example, finalizing work in China, in which we are doing work that responded more to providing inputs to China's new five year national energy plan rather than being an exercise for the water sector. We also recently completed some work in South Africa. We never established our concrete indicator saying "we need to influence countries." We're more on the *technical* side, making sure that we have this methodology well enough established and well designed, so that anyone can read it and apply it.

On the advocacy side, it was this issue of being a part of the dialogue with the energy sector. That has happened because we were also part of, for example, networks established by the US DOE and others. We were always part of these exercises with some of these larger energy producers on the topics.

By invitation? Were they coming to you?

Yeah.

It sounds like there was not a huge challenge in engaging stakeholders. Is that accurate to say?

No, it was in the beginning. Even within the Bank, we had this idea, and we had to work very closely with the energy colleagues to ensure that water was no longer perceived as not being an issue to deal with in planning and investment decisions. Initially, every time you tried to engage with the sector, you would get a response that implied that the issue of access to water would not be a problem to consider.

We were very lucky that at some point, in the work that we started in South Africa that Shell Oil was undertaking an exercise on the Nexus and we were invited to participate. This helped to raise awareness of the issue. At the same time,

Abengoa, which is a large renewable energy and water company from Spain, was also quite keen on the topic because they were facing some water limitations in projects that they were designing in Northern Africa. They immediately saw the opportunity of partnering with us and they really helped awareness of us grow globally because Abengoa would open doors with major energy players all over the world.

We started to function as a bit of a sounding board. We were advanced on some things, both on the technical and the advocacy side, and we would inform them and be part of their dialogues, but it was not an easy process. It really took two to three years before things started opening up. When we launched Thirsty Energy, it was at the World Energy Summit in Abu Dhabi. We launched it in an *energy* event, not a water event.

With the success that you've seen now in energy and bridging the gap there, do you have any clues as to how to bring in the agricultural sector at this point? Is that even on the radar? What's your strategy with agriculture going forward?

There's a whole discussion that started almost a year ago in the Bank on how to advance our initiative. We've done a couple of more upstream – and for us upstream means more regional or more general assessments – using what is called an integrated assessment model tool from the University of Maryland, that looks at the three issues – water, food, and energy. We are finalizing an assessment for North Africa, and we did some work on water security that also included food and energy for Latin America last year.

Much more upstream, much more broad is the question, "How do you balance water, energy, and food activity in a region?" It's tough for us because usually, in the context of the Bank, we have to ensure that these exercises are useful for *national* planning or investment designs, infrastructure and investment designs. But this is more analytical work at a *regional* scale. It was an initial type of exercise. The idea is eventually to delve deeper with similar instruments, but looking more at *national* planning. You can assess, for example, whether the national sector plans, because they are drafted and formulated in isolation without any correlation or synergies across sectors, whether you have enough capacity to fulfill all of the objectives of this different, very discreet, siloed sector-based plans when you look at the Nexus approach.

You have an agricultural plan and you have an energy plan, and you have a water plan. They may make a lot of sense if you look at each one of them in isolation, independently. They may *not* make a lot of sense when you try to combine the three, and really try to understand whether there is water to fulfill *all* of the plans: whether there's enough space for agriculture to grow as planned, or enough space for energy to grow as planned, because of potential constraints in water.

That's the same problem we have here. We have all our separate silos going on in the federal level. Agriculture doesn't talk to energy.

Exactly. They don't talk to each other but they plan anyway, particularly in developing countries. They come up with something like, "We're going to increase agricultural area by 100,000 hectares, and we're going to get this amount of water." If you ask them, "Where is the water coming from? Do you have the rights for the water?" their response is, "Oh, well, yeah, we'll get it."

Well, in some areas you won't. We looked at basins in South Africa where you have today 98 percent of the water already completely allocated, so you cannot ask for 3 percent more. It's just not there.

This kind of thinking is what we try to bring to the discussion, but it's very hard, again, because each sector is planning in isolation. They have their own policies and influences, and they are powerful contributors to growth and development.

What are the thoughts that you think need to be brought to the surface regarding your strategy, or the challenges, or what's ahead, or how to change awareness?

In the water sector we like to think that water is at the center of everything, but you really have to understand that we're only a very small player in these big economic plans against powerful sectors, so we really need to change the discourse of our narrative. It's no longer about "You should not be using water," because you will still use it, and you will still use it for growth and development, and also for social issues.

You have to provide water supply and sanitation to the population. But when you engage with these sectors your strategies should change quite drastically. It's no longer about, "You have to use our water balances or our tools to understand your constraints." It's always about constraints instead of opportunities. And that's part of the message that we try to change. It's no longer, "You use too much water." Well, they're going to keep on using the amount of water, so you might as well try to make that water much more efficiently allocated, or its use a bit better. And identify the financial gains to the industry of doing so.

It's a matter of changing a bit of the narrative. It's not always water-centric, it's about understanding how the other sectors work, plan, and decide. They have their own language, their own nomenclature. We have to understand much better how *they* operate.

How do you increase the valuation of water in their eyes? It's easy to put a value on kilowatt hours of energy generated, but how . . . it feels like water is playing catch-up to the rest of the mature industries.

Yeah, obviously. The valuation exercise is a completely different animal in these discussions. Usually what happens is in this planning framework, you're using the price of water currently being used in *that particular* basin, in that particular region. When we get into the valuation aspect, that is much more complex, because you're get into understanding the *opportunity* costs of a resource.

When looking at the opportunity cost, we illustrate the economic value of that drop of water be it in agriculture, in urban, in energy. Then you get into this aspect of valuation across sectors, and valuation for society as a whole . . . very tough. And you need to incorporate also the externalities into these valuation exercises. Not a simple process when we have other considerations rather than only economic costs.

Nexus solutions and livelihoods – job creation

One of the essential aspects of the Nexus stress that is not typically called out is how livelihoods are impacted – positively and negatively. Biggs et al. provide this linkage and simple graphics to align the Nexus with the overarching target of the SDGs to "free humanity from poverty and hunger as a matter of urgency."[9]

Biggs et al. recommend that it is "crucial to consider livelihoods more explicitly when presenting a set of global targets to achieve future sustainable development of society as a whole."[10] The authors propose an integrated framework to ensure that livelihoods be explicitly encapsulated within Nexus thinking. This framework enables conceptual and practical examination of human demand and natural resource supply within a system to ensure socio-ecological resilience and promote sustainable solutions for livelihoods through identifying Nexus synergies and tradeoffs (Figure 5.6).

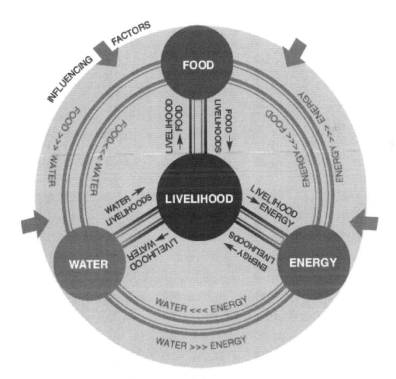

Figure 5.6 **Environmental livelihood security**

Source: Adapted from, Eloise Biggs et al., "Sustainable Development and the Water–Energy–Food Nexus: A Perspective on Livelihoods," *Environmental Science & Policy,* no. 54, December 2015: 389–397.

The authors of this book (Will and Greg) believe that *building an ecosystem of stakeholders to solve Nexus challenges and quantifying livelihood creation (moving people out of poverty) is an essential aspect of any Nexus solution.*

Nexus solutions and visualizing scenarios

A very recent article raises an important aspect of how to activate Nexus solutions – building scenarios.[11] The article presents "how participatory scenario-building processes can create space for dialogue amongst stakeholders with differing knowledge, experience, priorities, and political perspectives."

The article illustrates the success of this approach from case studies in Ethiopia and Rwanda by deploying a "Nexus toolkit." The case studies are focused on Nexus interactions at the landscape scale, for example, between charcoal production, food production, and environmental systems. The key conclusion by the authors is, "that participatory scenario-building processes that facilitate engagement beyond technical aspects to include social, economic and political concerns provide a valuable space for discussing and negotiating development pathways that are sustainable both biophysically and socio-economically."[12]

Other conclusions from this article include:

- By building capacity amongst stakeholders to maintain a quantitative "Nexus toolkit," it has a better chance of informing decision-making and for supporting the development of more technically refined analyses of alternative decisions and management strategies.
- The intrinsic complexity of the Nexus, particularly in relation to the charcoal sector, underlines the need for effective engagement between expert and non-expert stakeholders in order to understand biophysical interlinkages between resources and resource flows and social interactions between different actors in the socio-ecological system and landscape.
- Stakeholder engagement is also essential for building and negotiating solutions around how to better coordinate decision-making and management across sectors, for the

purpose of sustainable and equitable development. However, achieving effective engagement between expert and non-expert stakeholders can be a substantial challenge, due to varying levels of knowledge and understanding amongst actors with divergent and often entrenched, interests, and power to influence decision-making.

- A quantitative Nexus toolkit is needed, based upon the dynamic linking of a water and biomass modeling software tool – Water Evaluation and Planning (WEAP) – with an energy and climate modeling software tool – Long-range Energy Alternatives Planning (LEAP).

Now imagine coupling this approach with simple data visualization tools such as Tableau to illustrate – on a real time basis – the potential tradeoffs and solutions to the Nexus stress?

Final thought

Resource scarcity drives innovation. While we typically frame innovation as a technology opportunity, this dramatically limits our menu of solutions. We have found that innovation is thriving when we examine how the golden triangle ecosystem is driving innovative solutions and more importantly derailing our business-as-usual scarcity trajectory.

Most debates or negotiations related to resources (in particular water) start with the premise, on one or both sides of the table, of more – how can one user, conservationist, country, farmer, or industry get more for their own use? Thus the discussion begins with a state of conflict, with solutions driven by someone getting less of a given resource.

This concept of "more" is prevalent throughout most of society. What politician does not speak of more development, more jobs? What investor does not expect more profit? What industry does not want to grow its business?

Growth cannot be infinite and many places will face difficult choices. The authors hope this book helps lead to solutions that shift the discussion to bending demand to meet supplies and a contribution to well-being.

These are exciting times and we are confident that "business as usual" will not create the scarcity we project. Instead we believe innovation, broadly, will create abundance for all.

Notes

1 Roosevelt, Eleanor, quoted in BrainyQuote.com, https://www.brainyquote. com/quotes/quotes/e/eleanorroo100940.html, accessed November 10, 2017.

2 W2.vatican.va, Laudato si' (24 May 2015) Francis, http://w2.vatican.va/ content/francesco/en/encyclicals/documents/papa-francesco_20150524_ enciclica-laudato-si.html, accessed May 2, 2017.

3 Christiane Z. Peppard, "Hydrology, Theology, and Laudato Si'", *SAGE Journals*, Vol. 77, Issue 2, 2016.

4 Will Sarni, *Beyond the Energy–Water–Food Nexus: New Strategies for 21st Century Growth*, Dō Sustainability, 2015.

5 Eamonn Kelly. *Business Ecosystems Come of Age*, Deloitte University Press, 2015.

6 James Moore, "Predators and Prey: A New Ecology of Competition," *Harvard Business Review*, May–June, 1993.

7 Ibid.

8 Ibid.

9 Eloise M. Biggs, et al., "Sustainable Development and the Water–Energy–Food Nexus: A Perspective on Livelihoods," *Environmental Science & Policy*, no. 54, December 2015: 389–397.

10 Ibid.

11 Oliver W. Johnson, and Louise Karlberg, "Co-exploring the Water-Energy-Food Nexus: Facilitating Dialogue through Participatory Scenario Building," *Frontiers of Environmental Science*, May 2017.

12 Ibid.

CLOSING REMARKS

by Anders Berntell, Executive Director,
2030 Water Resources Group

As the authors of this book presents in Chapter 1, the challenges related to increasing demands for different uses of water versus a limited supply are daunting. 2030 WRG presented the estimate of a 40 percent gap between demand and supply in the report *Charting Our Water Future* in 2009. More recent reports have come up with different estimates for specific sectors that point in the same direction. A large part of the projected demand for water in 2030 will be for increased agricultural needs. Agriculture already accounts for 70 percent of total average water consumption worldwide. By 2030, food production will have to increase by 50 percent to meet the needs of a growing population. The International Energy Agency projects that water demand for energy generation and production will increase by 85 percent by 2035. In addition, increased urbanization leads to increasing urban water demands, per capita and in total, and on top of this we also have the effects of climate change, in many regions leading to decreasing water availability.

My perception is that the private sector earlier than many governments realized the risks and challenges this situation will lead to, for themselves as companies, but also for the wider economy and for opportunities for continued growth and development as such. This has been manifested for example in the WEF Annual Global Risk reports as well as in the CDP water disclosure reports.

The authors of this book both come from within the private sector, and reflect on their experiences through the lens of that private sector perspective.

For me, it is the opposite. My own background is in Water Resource Management within the public sector; implementing existing legislation, developing new public policies and legislation, nationally as well as internationally. This is normally something that is done internally, within the public administration, or sometimes after consultation with stakeholders, primarily academia and NGOs.

Many of us in the public sector, but also within academia and the NGO communities were skeptical about the private sector, their role and their impact, they were normally seen as part of the problem, contributing to the challenges we were facing.

My own experience of the international discussion on water started primarily when I was representing the Swedish Ministry for Environment as its Water Director in many of the international meetings and negotiations on water, from 1995–2002.

Initially, the only private sector participation in such negotiations at the global level was through the big international water utility companies. At the regional and EU levels I also experienced the participation of other private sector representatives in particular from manufacturing industry who were opposing stricter regulations on water quality standards etc. within the EU legislation.

However, when the water–food–energy Nexus discussions started to become more prominent, some of the water using/water dependent companies, in particular from the food and beverage sector, sometimes also the mining or energy sectors, got involved in those discussions. The authors are referring to the Bonn conference, and that might have been one of the starting points.

In 2002, I became the executive director of SIWI, where one of the main responsibilities was to organize the annual World Water Week in Stockholm. When joining, I was struck by the lack of private sector representatives in the World Water Week. It had mainly representatives from water specialists in academia and NGOs and water professionals from governments and other public entities.

Since I had earlier, within the context of the water–food–energy discussions, experienced the knowledge and insights as well as experience that some of these water using private sector companies had on primarily the water resource challenges, I wanted them to become more involved in the discussions of the World Water

Week in Stockholm. SIWI therefore started to actively reach out to them, and arrange seminars where the private sector was given an opportunity to present their experiences, views, and solutions to the challenges we were facing. The purpose was to engage them in discussions with representatives from the regular participants at the World Water Week, and vice versa.

In many cases these companies at that time had a higher level of understanding of the effects of water resource challenges had on our economies therefore on our societies as such but also on the environment and functioning of water dependent ecosystems than what many governments had at the same time. They realized that there was a direct relationship between water, the lack of it or the deterioration of its quality, and the operations of the companies' activities, its facilities and its supply chain, and thereby also a great risk that this would eventually affect the balance sheet of the company.

I remember that I hoped that we would be able to create the same level of understanding of that relationship for countries as such, explaining the relationship between water and the overall economic situation and performance of countries, its effects on GDPs and the risks that water could become a constraint for future economic growth and development for the country.

SIWI did some early and preliminary attempts to emphasize this relationship, for example in the report *Making Water a Part of Economic Development: The Economic Benefits of Improved Water Management and Services* (2005) which was presented by the governments of Norway and Sweden to the session on water within the UN Commission for Sustainable Development at that time.

A much more thorough and to my knowledge the only comprehensive attempt in this direction was later made by OECD and GWP in the 2015 report *Securing Water, Sustaining Growth,* a report of the GWP/OECD Task Force on Water Security and Sustainable Growth, with the main authors being Claudia Sadoff, Jim Hall, and David Grey.

The participation by water using private sector continued to increase at the WWW during my time at SIWI, but in my view is still far too low. One private sector that we in particular would need a stronger participation from is the financial sector, given the relatively low level of private sector investments in water in general, compared to many other sectors.

In 2012, after 10 years at SIWI, I decided to join the 2030 WRG as its first Executive Director. As has been described in Chapter 4, up until that time it had been hosted at the World Economic Forum, but was moved to IFC (International Finance Cooperation, a part of the World Bank Group) during the first half of 2012, which was also when I came onboard.

The reason I decided to take on the challenge of leading the work of 2030 WRG was primarily because I had become convinced that the only way we could effectively work to address the water resource challenges we were facing was by involving the water using private sector. In many ways their activities have been and still are a significant part of the problem, because of their abstraction of water or their discharge of waste(water) that affects the quality of that water. I had however become convinced that they could be brought onboard to become part of the solution instead, in particular because of their dependency on that water, its volumes or its quality but also because of their knowledge about how their own impact could be reduced, within their own facilities, in their supply chain, or in the regions or river basins where they were located.

I had been involved in many discussions on but also the concrete implementation of IWRM, internationally as well as in Sweden. In accordance with the Dublin principles, which are the original foundation of the IWRM concept, Principle 2 states that: "Water development and management should be based on a participatory approach, involving users, planners and policy-makers at all levels".

Never had I however experienced the participation of the water using private sector in the implementation of IWRM anywhere. Water users were normally defined as the civil society, NGOs, and citizen representatives or public utilities.

In the first phase of 2030 WRG, when still hosted at WEF, the approach for a country engagement was basically to send in a team of international consultants to perform a hydro-economic analysis of the country, with a particular emphasis on the marginal cost-curve methodology to identify the most cost-effective interventions and to facilitate a dialogue with stakeholders and the government about what policy options that should be prioritized. The work and the consultation were normally performed within a relatively short time, and included a number of stakeholder consultations in workshops and various meetings. As a result, the government normally agreed to some kind of strategic plan or policy document for the country's water resource management. The task of the secretariat of the 2030 WRG was thereafter to convince the government of the need to implement these policy recommendations.

The experience we realized when during 2012 and 2013 was however that the practical implications of many of these recommendations were not fully understood or internalized by all the relevant stakeholders in the country, neither within the government itself, nor within the civil society or private sector. The approach had been too much top-down, and the conclusions were not internalized by the various groups that needed to be onboard. As a result, after changes in governments after elections etc., the original policy recommendations were sometimes discarded, neglected, or forgotten.

When we started to engage in new countries, after 2012, we therefore chose another approach, much inspired by the experience from our work in South Africa at that time, where a more institutionalized and structured platform for engaging with all stakeholders had been set up. This had proven to be a very useful tool to ensure a strong commitment by all partners, with dual and strong leadership in the process by both government and private sector.

We still consider that a hydro-economic analysis, which sometimes also can include a cost-effectiveness study of various interventions, is a very useful tool to present the water challenges and what can be done to address them. In particular for participants that are from other sectors than water, including for key decision-makers in government and private sector. However, with the new approach, the ownership of the analysis and the results thereof becomes much stronger than earlier.

Furthermore, the multi-stakeholder platform becomes instrumental in prioritizing and developing the concrete proposal for various interventions: policies, programs, and projects that will be implemented later on by the respective stakeholders. This structured multi-stakeholder process also ensures that all relevant implications of such interventions are discussed in an open and transparent manner, since all groups do have a seat at the table: government, private sector, and civil society/NGOs. This enables us to discuss and address potential social, economic, environmental, and political implications of any intervention, not only the cost/benefit aspects. When all relevant partners are involved, including those that will be involved in the financing of certain programs, or government agencies responsible for the implementation of other polices or regulations, the step towards implementation becomes much shorter than what otherwise would be the case.

There are several organizations and initiatives that are promoting or implementing water stewardship in various forms, 2030 WRG is far from alone. What I find is one of the strongest values of the 2030 WRG approach however is the very strong emphasis of the role of the government in this work. We would never engage in a country without a formal invitation from senior representatives (ministers, prime ministers, or presidents) of that government, and a belief from our side that there is a genuine and strong commitment from that government, combined with a capacity to deliver. Therefore, we also always engage at the country level as such, or in the case of federal states where water management and governance is delegated to the state level, at that level instead.

Other organizations and initiatives might choose other starting points for their engagement, such as an individual company or group of companies facing certain challenges in a river basin etc. I believe that different approaches are needed to address the multitude of challenges we are facing, and that there is room for them all, and even synergies that can be more effectively explored between them. With the strong convening power that the 2030 WRG represents, including through the roles of many of its partners at the global level, individual companies, WEF, the World Bank, and IFC, we have in many countries/states been able to create very strong and powerful multi-stakeholder platforms, where different parts of government are represented, including various line-ministries such as on energy, agriculture, mining, industry, etc. (not only water) but also other critical parts of the government such as ministry of finance/economy, central planning etc. In many cases there is also a close connection to the prime minister's or president's office, and sometimes the steering boards of such multi-stakeholder platforms are also chaired by such representatives, not by the water ministries themselves. This shows an important realization of waters fundamental role for the country as such, for its future growth and development, beyond the responsibility of the Ministry of Water alone, creating an effective instrument for addressing the water–food–energy Nexus and beyond.

So, have we been successful in this endeavor? Yes, I believe so; out of the 13–14 countries we have engaged in, we have at this time established structured multi-stakeholder platforms in 10 of them with over 500 partners actively participating in the work. They have together:

- Decided on 60 areas of priority for their work
- Developed 71 concept notes to concretize those areas
- Developed these concept notes into 53 final proposals
- Set up preparatory arrangements for implementation for 39 of these proposals
- Seen the full implementation on the ground for 19 of these programs

This has been achieved over the five-year period of hosting within IFC, with a continued increase of number of countries over those years, where some of them have only been operational for the last one or two years, and have therefore not reached as far as others.

Have we been able to address the water–food–energy Nexus challenges effectively?

If one would have the ambition to reduce both water and energy consumption while at the same time producing more food, I believe the only examples we can provide are those that focuses on increased water use efficiency in irrigated agriculture. We do have several such programs being developed, or already implemented in for example India, Bangladesh, South Africa, Kenya, Tanzania, Mexico, and Peru.

Other programs might have a more limited scope with regards to the Nexus, addressing for example only water and energy consumption. Reducing water leakage in the municipal water supply systems, increasing water use efficiency within manufacturing industries or increasing the reuse and recycling of wastewater from municipalities or industries would all have that effect, with various degrees of efficiency. Many such programs are also already being implemented or developed in several of our countries in all the regions.

However, in my view, the most important and probably most long-lasting effect of our work will probably be the creation of platforms in countries where the public-private and civil society can start building trust between them, and work together to address the Nexus challenges (and beyond) that affect their country, people, ecosystems, and economy.

INDEX

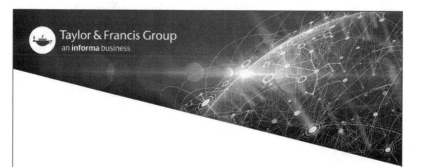